WOMAN IN
PRE-COLUMBIAN
AMERICA

THE IMAGE OF WOMAN

THE IMAGE OF WOMAN

FERDINAND ANTON

WOMAN IN PRE-COLUMBIAN AMERICA

ABNER SCHRAM

NEW YORK

DISTRIBUTION: UNIVERSE BOOKS, NEW YORK
GEORGE PRIOR PUBLISHERS, LONDON

Translated from the German by Marianne Herzfeld,
revised by Professor George A. Shepperson.
We also want to thank Miss J. Gibson for her assistance

Published in the United States of America
by Abner Schram (A Division of Schram Enterprises)
1860 Broadway, New York, N.Y. 10023
Distributed by Universe Books
381 Park Avenue South, New York, N.Y.
ISBN 0-8390-0128-2

Published in England by Abner Schram, London
in association with George Prior Publishers Ltd.
Rugby Chambers, 2 Rugby Street, London WCIN 3QU

TABLE OF CONTENTS

INTRODUCTION

It was the image of an unknown woman—called "pretty lady" by archaeologists—that marked the start of the development of art in Old America; and it was Malintzin, later known as Doña Marina, without whose help Hernán Cortés could not so easily have conquered Mexico and large parts of Central America.

A symbolic and rather strange scene heralded the tragic decline of the high Indian civilizations. During a temporary landing on the south-eastern part of the Gulf of Mexico, Cortés arranged in the presence of Indian dignitaries a spectacle to impress the Indians. A mare and a hot-blooded stallion were the actors, both animals unknown and therefore mysterious to the Indians. Loudly neighing and stamping his hoofs the passionate quadruped rushed into the assembly as soon as he scented the mare, which the Spaniards had hidden. The spectacle was impressive. The foreign soldiers quieted the wild animal with Spanish words, bound to sound like spells to Indian ears. The chief of the Indians thereupon presented the Spaniards with twenty young women, among them Malintzin, whom Cortés chose for himself to serve him both as interpreter and as mistress.

The other Indian women were given as presents to the captains and other officers. There is no memorial in today's Mexico of Malintzin, who collaborated with the Spaniards and became most important for their later enterprises. Only an extinct volcano bears her name.

The linguistic gap between Spanish and Nahuatl, the vernacular of the Aztecs, was bridged for Cortés through the Maya language by Jerónimo de Aguilar, who had been stranded on the coast of Yucatán in 1511 during the first expedition under the Spaniard Valdivia, was made prisoner by the Maya Indians and learned their language. When he heard that the Spaniards were trying another attack, he escaped to join the armies of Cortés. Malintzin also knew a Maya dialect. Originally sold as a slave to the *kazike* (chief) who gave her to Cortés, she came from a village near Coazacualco, where both the vernacular of the Aztecs and that of the neighboring Maya Indians were spoken.

Later the chronicler Bernal Díaz del Castillo wrote about Malintzin: "God has blessed her by liberating her from the worship of idols. Had one made her the ruler over all Mexico she would not have wanted it, because there was not anything in all the world which she valued more than to serve her lord Cortés ... As Jerónimo de Aguilar understood the vernacular of Yucatán [Maya

Page out of a series of four pages with scenes depicted shortly after the Spanish conquest; it shows Malintzin and Cortés at the latter's negotiations with Indian dignitaries (Codex, private property, Los Angeles)

Yucateco], which was similar to Malintzin's, these two people got on well together, so that Aguilar could afterwards explain everything to Cortés in the language of Castile. This was a good beginning for our conquest ... I wanted to explain this, as without Doña Marina [Malintzin] we would not have understood the vernacular of New Spain [Mexico]."

Bernal Díaz was the first to refer in European literature to the proverbial faithfulness of the Indian woman and her total submission to her lord and master.

Early America would not have been courted so much by suitors, had not the earliest of these taken it for the rich Indies or the legendary China, of which Marco Polo had reported in Europe one hundred and fifty years earlier. At the Isthmus of Panama the conquerors for the first time held gold in their hands and heard the promising legend of the gilded king and of the great treasures in the countries further south. This continent was to bring immense riches to all the reigning houses of Europe, while its aborigines were to suffer calamities past description.

Most Europeans and North Americans see in the Indians a race all of whose members look alike, unchanged since the Spanish conquest. These views are mistaken. The Indians differ greatly from tribe to tribe and from country to country.

According to Paul Rivet, at the time of Christopher Columbus the Indians may have totalled between forty and forty-five millions. This French etymologist proved that there were 123 linguistic families with separate vernaculars; and there were no blood relationships between them.[1]

The people in the New World also showed innumerable different features, their religions many different traits; habits and customs varied greatly. The reader has to realize that the variety of the Indian civilizations, which had evolved independently of non-American civilizations, represents in fact a "New World." Most of our information on the earliest cultures of the southern hemisphere derives not from written records but from the treasures of the graves—those that, more or less by chance—escaped the treasure hunters, or *huaqueros*.[2]

Ancient Mexico

In the highlands of Mexico, which held back the savage nomads coming from the north, the cultivation of maize was apparently started about 5000 B.C.; it was to provide the second largest item of the world's food production. There, too, are to be found the first witnesses to a great artistic past, the "Pretty Ladies of Tlatilco" (Ill. 1–12). Here also is Cuicuilco, the "Site of Song and Dance," and the pyramid of Cholula, probably the oldest cultic building in America, in cubic content the largest pyramid of the world. In the first six centuries A.D. there flourished the spiritual centre Teotihuacán, the "Place of Origin of the Gods," a town larger than classical Athens or ancient Rome (Ill. 62). The warlike Toltecs, who founded Tula, the "Town of Reeds," were a predominant power from about the tenth until the mid-fourteenth century when the Aztecs came to the foreground of the Mexican stage.

In the northwest there lived (and still live today) the Tarascan Indians, who were hereditary enemies of the Aztecs and denied them armed help when the Spaniards invaded the country. They fraternized with the enemy and offered the Conquistadores not only warriors, but also their daughters and sisters as a special proof of friendship, which made the Spaniards their *tarahcue*, or "sons- or brothers-in-law." From this word the name of the Tarascans is derived.

Further south, in the fertile highland valley of Oaxaca, was the home of the Zapotecs, noted for the vast scale of their building activities. Their neighbors to the north were the Mixtecs, who were outstanding craftsmen, working in clay and gold (Ill. 57). They wrote in pictures, signs and symbols, developing hieroglyphs in a first step toward a phonetic alphabet. The Aztecs adopted these hieroglyphs, which have been preserved in "Folding Books" (strips of stag leather, folded like an accordion), but the Aztecs developed them no further. The Latin letters of the conquerors displaced the ancient hieroglyphs, but some picture-scripts survived. Knowledge of the hieroglyphs was never disseminated outside the priestly class and with the decline of its power, the art fell into oblivion. Except for records of a few births and important marriages like that of Princess "Seven Flower," which took place in A.D. 692, the surviving scripts tell us nothing about the lives of the women of ancient America (Ill. 59).

Central America

The civilization of the so-called Olmecs, the "People from the Rubberland," stems from a still remoter past. The date, 32 B.C., is recorded on one of their monu-

8

ments. The altars in the centres of religious worship at La Venta, on the southern shore of the Gulf of Mexico, show mothers carrying in their arms helmeted, gnome-like children, known as the "Jaguar Children" (Ill. 18, 21). The civilization of the Olmecs (from about 600 B.C. to A.D. 200) showed a remarkable degree of specialization. An élite was formed here in a comparatively short time, which then extended its influence not only to the highlands of Mexico, but to all Central America. Although there are as yet no conclusive proofs to confirm whether the Olmecs were a people or only an intellectual élite, yet it is certain that the earliest known script and calendar system in the New World originated from La Venta, the intellectual centre of this seminal civilization.

The most fertile soil for the spread of Olmec culture was that of the Maya Indians. The area between the Gulf of Mexico, the Gulf of Honduras and the Pacific Ocean has often been called the Egypt of the New World. It is still today the home of almost two million Maya Indians. The Mayas developed a system of hieroglyphs more advanced than that of the Mixtecs. Of those that have been deciphered (less than 40 percent), most are concerned with the calendar system. Thus, from hieroglyphs incised in monuments or painted on vessels of clay, we have been able to translate exact dates, but nothing concerning the dignitaries or gods represented (Ill. 73, 76).

The "Gold-lands"

The "Gold-lands" proper, South Nicaragua, Costa Rica, Panama and Colombia, have proved bridges as well as barriers between the two centres of the old-Indian high civilizations. The Atlantic side of the continent, densely forested, humid and rainy, provided a home for a small, half-nomadic population of Indians.

On the southern coast of the Lake of Nicaragua and on the peninsula of Nicoya (Costa Rica), lived the tribes of the Chorotegs and Nicaraos. These tribes left ceramics as multi-coloured as they were imaginative (Ill. 93–95), their shape and the motifs pointing to a pantheon of supernatural and fantastic beings. There are no signs of the beginning of script, nor any traces that the high civilization of the neighboring Mayas was taken as a guide.

In Colombia and in Panama, the main bearers of pre-Spanish civilization were the Chibcha tribes. Chief among these were the Muiscas, who settled in the high valleys in the district of Bacatá, the later Bogotá. There, in the *tierra fría*, the eastern Cordilleras, about 2,000 to 3,000 metres above sea level, their civilization evolved. Notwithstanding their highly regarded art, they remained at the first stage of a barbaric authoritarian civilization, under the leadership of chiefs and Shaman priests.

It was in Colombia and North Ecuador that, as shown by recent finds, the beginnings of the art of ceramics can be traced as far back as the period between 4000 and 3000 B.C. The archaeology of this region is still in its infancy. In the upper part of the Magdalena Valley of Colombia, there are the remains of a very old civilization, called after the present-day village San Agustín, and noted for its remarkable stone sculpture (Ill. 97). There are more than three hundred monumental sculptures, representing anthropomorphic and zoomorphic beings with asexual features and the faces of beasts of prey.

Peru

The remarkable condition of preservation of ancient Peruvian artifacts is due to two circumstances: to the practices of the cults of the dead and the care given to it (as in ancient Egypt many offerings were deposited with the dead in their graves); and, secondly, to the favourable climate. There is hardly any rainfall on the Peruvian coast; moreover, the soil is rich in sodium nitrate, so that, especially in the south, even such delicate things as artifacts made of feathers, woven materials and wood-carvings have survived (Ill. 101, 107, 108, 109, 112). We find here examples of the handiwork of women to which there is hardly anything comparable elsewhere in the world.

From among the large number of the various civilizations which preceded the reign of the Incas in old Peru, the Dionysian civilization of Moche at the northern coast is worth mentioning in connection with the theme of this book. The Mochicas have been called the Greeks of South America because they did not hesitate to attribute human and animal traits to the gods and demons of their Olympus. Nor did they scruple to retain, in a library of clay sculptures, reports of their most intimate human relations, and to add items of this library as offerings to the dead in their graves (Ill. 104, 110, 111). The civilizations of Paracas and Nazca on the southern coast of Peru demonstrated a talent in the use of ornament and colour.

The realism of the north was replaced in the south by symbolism which survives in the wonderful *mantas* (shrouds) (Ill. 109, 112). About two hundred years before the Spanish conquest, a small élite group systematically subjugated the other peoples of the region. In its final phase, the state of the Incas was able, by means of its strong military power and organized hierarchy of officials, to extend its influence over a territory covering thirty-seven degrees of latitude.

Inca history can be traced only through oral tradition preserved at the time of the conquest, because no hieroglyphic or phonetic system of writing had developed. What we have from the Incas is a script of knotted strings *(quipu)*, a numerical system which enabled the state to keep track of every citizen and of the distribution of goods and cultivated lands throughout the empire.

Written Reports from the Time of the Conquest

When in the early 16th century the Spanish conquistadores left their fleet at anchor and advanced slowly but irresistibly on the continent, only scanty reports reached Europe, the conquerors contenting themselves with brief records of their deeds in their logbooks or in brief descriptions in letters to their patrons.

Frequently the mercenary soldiers who joined the expeditions could neither read nor write. Of the five Spaniards who were the first to see Cuzco, the capital of the Inca empire, called the navel of the world, not one left a single line.

More exact and systematic recording of information began on April 22, 1519, the day Cortés landed near Veracruz and reported on his enterprise in detailed letters to the Emperor Charles V. Missionaries followed the soldiers. The report by Fra Bernardino de Sahagún, a Franciscan monk, on pre-Spanish Mexico are of the greatest value. This monk, who came to Mexico in 1529, was far ahead of his time in the field research methods he employed. In collecting information, it was not Sahagún himself but the person whom he was interrogating who was the narrator in the foreground of his accounts. He was able to assemble around himself a large number of Indians and to teach them the Latin alphabet. He let them tell him in their vernacular, the Nahuatl, everything they knew of the old gods, the priests and kings, their various qualities, their different ranks and the badges which show all these. Even the advantages and disadvantages experienced by individuals in the various professions, the judicial system, the strict religious worship, the education of children and the lot of women are described in detail in this huge catalogue, the *Codex Florentino*, which was not to be finished before 1569. Fortunately for historical research, this manuscript was temporarily lost and thereby escaped the ban of the Inquisition. A later edition translated by Sahagún himself is called the *Historia general de las Cosas de la Nueva España;* it differs considerably in certain important points from the original. It shows all too clearly which subjects, tabooed by the priests, Sahagún had to avoid in his research.[3]

It was the misfortune of the Indian cultures of South America to be conquered by the European powers Spain and Portugal, which opposed the advanced ideas of their time. Reports from the New World are hampered by prejudice, taboos, and gaps in understanding. Beginning with the earliest sources (accounts written by monks) woman is prejudiced through her inferior position. But with the *Codex Florentino* by Sahagún, the *Codex Mendoza*, written by natives and commissioned for the Emperor Charles V by his namesake the Viceroy of Mexico in 1535, and the chronicle of the Indian Poma de Ayala, it has become possible to reconstruct among other things a picture of the duties and customs of women's everyday life.[4]

The earliest detailed accounts of the Mayas, *Relación de las cosas de Yucatán,*[5] were written in 1566 in self-justification by Bishop Diego de Landa, who was ordered back from America to Spain because of his outrages. "These people [the Mayas] use certain symbols and letters to write down in their books their ancient history and their dogmas. With the help of these letters, of drawings and of certain figures they can recount history, make it understandable to others and teach it. We found a large number of such books, and when we discovered that they did not contain anything but what clearly pointed to superstition and the lies of the devil, we burnt them all, to the deep vexation and regret of these people."

Europeans reared under the fanatic Inquisition, and always threatened by it, could hardly gauge the tremendous damage done by the burning of the books and by other destructive acts which the bishop had ordered. Of the large number of Maya manuscripts, then existing, only three escaped the flames of religious fanaticism

(Ill. 73, 76). The outstandingly beautiful pictography of this, the most intellectual civilization of pre-Columbian America, is the *Codex Dresdensis*, which is presently in the Sächsische Landesbibliothek at Dresden. It contains, among other things, a comparison of the revolutions of Venus and of the sun. The books of the Jaguar priests (Chilam Balam), written by Maya Indians, according to verbal traditions, approximately between 1600 and 1650, confirm some of the historical dates, but are difficult to understand owing to their mainly mythological contents.[6] Most of our information concerning this civilization comes, unfortunately, from the man who was himself responsible for the destruction of the original Indian documents, Diego de Landa. He describes the everyday life of the Indians, reports upon their habits and customs, and gives a partial key to the study of the Mayan calendar.

The few reports by Spaniards who were in the early colonial time in contact with the Chorotegs, Nicaraos and the Indians of Panama are skimpy; they mention women only where habits and usage are totally different from those of Spain. A notable chronicler, the soldier Pedro Cieza de León, described an event which he claimed took place in the region of the source of the Rio Sucio; perhaps he wanted to excite the imagination of the Europeans with regard to those exotic lands: "When" —so he writes—"Christians and Spaniards entered these valleys for the first time—and that included me and my companions—, a tall gentleman came to us of his own free will; he called himself Nabonúco. He brought three women with him, and when night came two of them stretched out on a mat or a carpet on the floor and a third lay at right angles to them to serve as a pillow. Then the Indian lay down lengthwise on their bodies and took by the hand another beautiful woman who had stayed behind with his people and who came forward only now. When the lawyer Juan de Vadillo saw them like that, he asked why the chief had brought this other woman, whom he was holding only by the hand. Looking him straight in the eye the Indian chief answered gently, 'So as to eat her,' and had Vadillo not come, he would certainly have done so. When Vadillo heard this, he asked in evident surprise: 'You really wanted to eat her, though she is your wife?' And the *kazike* replied: 'Yes, and the child, to which she is to give life, that too shall I eat.'"—It is hardly possible to say today to what extent the story was distorted by the lawyer, then still young, who later became a very trustworthy chronicler.[7] One thing, however, is certain: cannibalism was widespread among the aborigines of Colombia.

The Spaniards incited enemy tribes to fight each other and thereupon intervened. Tortures, blindings, decapitations were the order of the day. The soldiery left their traces everywhere. The conquest moved further and further south, always in the hope of finding "El Dorado," a kind of golden Cockaigne. At Christmas 1538, in the region of Cali, the Conquistadores met their compatriots who shortly before had taken possession of the mighty empire of the Incas and now marched northwards.

For the regions which the Spaniards called "Alto Perú" comprising the present-day Ecuador, Peru, Bolivia, North Chile and Northwest Argentina, the chronicles are again more numerous but also more contradictory. In many of them one can at once clearly detect a one-sided attitude. For instance, the Spaniard Sarmiento de Gamboa[8] described the Indians as mere barbaric heathens, while his contemporary, the Inca Garcilaso de la Vega,[9] tended to exaggerate in favour of the Indians, whose blood flowed in his veins. More objective is the detailed report on Peru by Cieza de León (mentioned above) who spent several decades there. The difference in interpreting one and the same event is shown by a particularly striking example: the description of the ancestry of the Incas by the above mentioned chroniclers:

Indian viewpoint:

I once asked my uncle about the beginning of the empire and he willingly explained it to me. "Keep well in your heart what I now shall tell you. You know that previously, in ancient times, the country was bare and empty and the people lived without morals, like wild beasts.

When the sun god, our father, saw this he took pity and sent from heaven one of his sons, Manco Capac, and one of his daughters, Mama Oello, so that men should recognize him as god and learn to live sensibly and lovingly together. From his two children men were also to learn how to build houses, to till the land and all the other arts of civilization.

He let his children descend to earth on a small island in the Lake of Titicaca, and gave them the choice of the direction in which to proceed. They were to settle down and found their empire only where they should succeed in driving the golden staff, which he gave them, easily into the ground; it was half an ell long and two fingers thick. He also said: 'If you succeed in taking these people under your sovereignty, then reign mercifully and justly over them. Act as a kind father treats his children, and as I my-

self treat the world; give it light to see, warmth against the cold, and fertility for the preservation of life. That is the reason why I make you the rulers of the country.' With this advice he dismissed the divine children. These then wandered from Lake Titicaca to the north, and tried to drive the staff into the soil, but failed to do so. When they came to the Cuzco Valley they rested south of the town, on Mount Anacanti, and there they succeeded in driving the staff so far into the ground that it disappeared. Then the first Inca said to his sister and wife: 'We shall settle here as this is also what our father wants us to do.'

They then assembled many people and instructed them in all arts and other activities. Manco Capac taught the men, and his sister-wife, the Queen, taught the women weaving and other crafts.

The benefits which the people of this valley received from the Incas inspired all the inhabitants of the valley and of the mountains to speak about them and to tell everyone of the blessings and the kindness which they received from the Incas. Many people therefore gathered so that the Inca in a short time had assembled so many warriors that he could extend his empire . . . "

Spanish viewpoint:

It is a thing worthy to be written down and certainly true, showing how these tyrannical and cruel Incas of Peru extended their general tyranny to the aborigines—we can easily learn this from history if we read it attentively.

This will also show the kind of treatment suffered by the people who were natives in these parts, and were forced, against their will and without their choice, into the mighty Inca empire. They were, as always, prepared to take up arms and to seek every opportunity to rise against the tyranny of the Incas and to free themselves from serfdom. It was not sufficient that each Inca imitated the tyranny of his father; he even tried to surpass it, and started again and again with the same oppression and with war, robbery, murder and theft, so that no one could state with good conscience that they had succeeded by honest means—neither has any of them ever peacefully acquired land. That was the reason why constantly some of the natives took up arms and rose against the Incas and their tyranny. Moreover it is worth recording that they (the Incas) were not satisfied with venting their evil inclinations and their horrible greed and tyranny upon the people alone, but that they also treated their own children, their brothers, their relations, even relations by blood, and their own laws and statutes equally badly and madly and with an unbelievable kind of inhumanity.

According to their customs and their tyrannical law, the eldest son was the legitimate heir of the empire of the Inca. But this law was usually violated, as I shall tell you. To begin with, Manco Capac, the first of the tyrants, who came from Tambotoco,

treated barbarously his brother Ayar Cache. He sent him to Tambotoco, but sent there also Tambo Chamcay to kill him, as he envied Ayar Cache's bravery and thought that because of this the people would be more attached to him. Afterwards when Manco Capac came to the Valley of Cuzco he tyrannized not only over the native people but also over those of Copali Mayta and Colum Chima, who also inhabited the valley, and who were his relatives, and of his rank, because they were Orejones (big ears).[10]

It might well be that because of their wickedness the Almighty let them be their mutual executioners . . .

On the one hand we have the sophisticated half-Spanish Inca Garcilaso de la Vega, who claimed an Inca princess as his mother, introducing his comprehensive history of the Incas with the ancient fable of the idealized origin of the Inca dynasty, and, on the other hand, a Spaniard attempting to justify the cruel conquest which directed his own hatred quite openly into his pen. Some of the historical information that we have from the Spanish chroniclers is prejudiced in other ways. For example, they tend to exaggerate when speaking of the numbers of human sacrifices or the number of their enemies. But when they speak of their own army, the numbers which they give are too small, and they frequently do not mention the large mass of auxiliaries from the ranks of the Indian population.

We come to know the men and especially the women of old America through the inanimate monuments left to us, through their art, their religion and the outlook which we can gather to have formed the basis of their traditions, their habits and their myths, legends and fables. The fables are stories founded on archaic religious conceptions, while the legends usually contain a historical nucleus, although embellished with poetical imagination.

Archaeological knowledge has made rapid progress in recent decades, making discoveries which enable us to draw a picture of the pre-Spanish civilizations. With the help of modern physics, chemistry and biology, the archaeologist now finds one new way after another to induce the relics of the past to speak. What once began with the examination of fossils and deposits has now developed into a science bringing to light what only lately seemed for ever lost in the twilight of the past.

Although the huge detailed mosaic showing the past of the New World is far from having been fully assembled, yet the corner pieces, helping to mark the outlines, have been set in place.

EARLIEST
CIVILIZATIONS

The soil of America exposes the evidence of the ancient civilizations that preceded the advanced ones, at times hesitantly but at times very liberally.

What we can say about the position of woman and her rights, about the outlook and the religion of the earliest inhabitants of America, is fragmentary. Only the offerings in the graves of the pre-classic civilization, preserved in large numbers thanks to the worship of the dead and the favourable climate, point to a high valuation of woman, which in later centuries was no longer so clearly to be seen.

Tlatilco

"Tlatilco" means, in the Nahuatl language, "the place where things are hidden." A rather typical pre-classic village-like settlement located in Mexico, Tlatilco is one of the oldest and most rewarding sites of prehistoric remains. Of particular interest was the discovery of a large number of charming small clay figures—"the Pretty Ladies of Tlatilco," as archaeologists called these grave offerings. The scholars estimate the ages of these figures at approximately 2500 to 3200 years (Ill. 1—13). They are almost exclusively representations of women, given to the dead to accompany them on their journey to the other world and "killed" (that is ritually broken) during the entombment. The small clay figures of neighboring valleys are often distinguished from one another only by the parts of the face round the eyes, and the delicately and neatly modelled hairdressing.

The picture of their inhabitants given us by Tlatilco and similar places, which makes the pre-classic period between Michoacán and El Salvador appear almost as a unity, is typical for the pre-theocratic period (about 3000–300 B.C.). The small ceramics show that the peasants wore no clothes. They lived in huts with walls of plaited reeds covered with clay, usually near lakes or rivers. They formed small village communities, planting maize (Indian corn), marrow, and chili, fattening small dogs and hunting sea birds and stags to enlarge as far as possible their modest diet. They had few possessions. The excavations showed tools of bone and stone, fishing nets, a few straw-mats, and, surprisingly, beds on four posts, an achievement which fell into disuse with their successors. There was not yet any organized caste of priests, but the small figures and masks give proof of the existence of shamans, probably some of them female.

Among the discoveries of Tlatilco are sculptures, chiefly figures of women or young girls, that seem surprisingly modern (Ill. 1, 7, 9). It is uncertain whether these offerings from the graves are fertility goddesses or dancers in the service of shamans, or perhaps simply revered women. Undoubtedly, however, the standard of physical beauty of those times is reflected in a sequence of nearly a thousand years. While in the region of Michoacán a full bosom seems to have been thought pleasing (Ill. 17), in Tlatilco the ideal evidently was broad wide hips and small maidenlike breasts (Ill. 4).

Innumerable beauty aids were already at the disposal of women: the face was painted with make-up obtained from plants and minerals; the body and the hair were dyed. Various artistically arranged coiffures stressed the individuality of the characters represented by the clay statuettes: among the thousands of clay figures and fragments, no individual example of artistic hairdressing is even once exactly repeated. The range of the hairdressing extends from the German "Gretchen" type with long plaits, or from fringes falling far on to the face, to high toupees recalling French caricatures of the Rococo period.

For the face and the body, ornaments shaped like spiral scrolls and painted ochre or vermillion were much favoured. The same colours were used also to dye and powder the hair; the strength and durability of the dyes can be gauged today by the antiquity of these finds from the graves. The excavations show yet another means used for beautifying: the front teeth of the most noble ladies were stopped with jade. That this extremely difficult and painful operation by stone-age dentists was done for beauty's sake, is attested to by the fact that many healthy teeth have been found on which it was performed: small vanities led even then to great sacrifices. The operations were performed with drills of obsidian or flint fragments. By using a long-lasting cement, the composition of which has only lately been discovered by a Scandinavian scientist, the jade bead was fixed in the tooth as a decoration for the mouth.

Clothes seemed less important to the ladies; when they were not quite naked, they wore very short skirts and sandals. In later cultures—the Mayan, for example—more importance was attached to garments and jewelry, which were meant to indicate their owner's status and relationship to the clans and tribes.

Had not tools of bone and stone been found together with male skeletons in the pre-classic graves, one could almost have envisaged a society of Amazons, since male representations are rare. The "pretty ladies" of the archaic period seem to bear witness to an early food-growers' civilization, in which the woman took an important religious and probably also social part.

Excavations in other regions, belonging to the same time, show an overwhelming majority of mother and child representations. Charm and female coquetry emanate from these small clay women; there are no sexual or obscene images. (In a few examples, however, the phallus is combined with female breasts or other parts of the female body.) Not only the sculptured figures, but also all the other ceramics, show the rapid growth of the artistic faculty of expression. Frequently bowls are shaped into artistically modelled objects, such as animals, fish or acrobats. The ceremonial vessels used in the service of the dead are particularly well and lovingly made.

Around 500 B.C. there is a change in the appearance of the cheerful dancers and ladies. Another culture had forced itself into the high-lying valleys of Mexico, bringing innovation of a fundamental nature. These innovators, the so-called "Olmecs," left their image in the graves of Tlatilco and other archaeological sites. The central figure of Olmec religion was a goddess of water and fertility, a combination of woman-mother and jaguar—presumably the animal whose qualities were most admired by men (Ill. 18).

The jaguar-people found in Tlatilco were made in the characteristic Olmec style, which had its centre further south, chiefly in the La Venta mangrove woods on the Gulf coast. Whether formed of clay or sculptured in stone, these figures, with their infantile proportions and sometimes gnomish features, show high artistic quality and differ from their realistic predecessors in their strong stylization. Often they wear a helmet-like head-dress and frequently also show other war-like traits. In the Mexican highlands, this type of figure, with its characteristic turned-up lips, is usually coated with a layer of a polished whiteish colour. Small stone figures made of jade or green serpentine show remnants of reddish paint obtained from cinnabar. The La Venta style, called after one of its places of discovery, spread quickly. It is distinguished by its special stylized features and its high artistic quality from the objects of the earlier farmers. It is found mostly in the graves of highly-placed persons. Since it spread so quickly over a wide area, it is difficult to say whether this was the result of the spread

14

of an idea or that of an armed conquest. The Olmec grave offerings and those influenced by Olmec ideas show signs of the beginning of a theocratic period. In the classical period of almost seven hundred years which was, as in nearly all high civilizations, greatly influenced by a priestly élite, we hardly ever find the woman as an individual, but as a goddess or the goddess's priestess.

Colima

One region in Mesoamerica[11] was not influenced by the so-called mother civilization of the Olmecs: the northwest coast of Mexico. Its inhabitants did not take part in the rise or decline of theocratic classicism. Their libraries of clay left behind in shaft-graves nearly 15 metres deep contain a whole human comedy. Discoveries in this region are in the highest degree folk-art: naive and gay and owing everything to spontaneous impressions. This art was introduced to history under the names of "Colima," "Jalisco," and "Nayarit," the present-day states of the Mexican Confederation where many of the discoveries were made.

The ceramics tell, in loving detail, of pregnancy and confinement, of children at their mothers' breast, and of the older ones enjoying their games. Nowhere in America has the theme "mother and child" been treated so often, so fervently, or so lovingly (Ill. 22, 30, 32, 33).

The austere rigidity of the theocratic type of art was unable to take hold here; perhaps the temperament of the people was too much at variance with the severe religious ideas of the neighboring regions.

Not burdened by religious dogmas, these ceramics present a circle of everyday happenings, often amusing, sometimes slipping into caricature or obscenity. Some are as forceful as works of expressionist art, and greatly impressive. Differences in social rank are shown only by the suggestion of a loin cloth, by the jewelry worn in ear and nose, and by the various kinds of tattooing on face and chest. Signs of social worries and of illnesses are also to be seen (Ill. 32, 33). These sculptures form a lasting memorial for the women whom they represent, and simultaneously for the unknown artists.

Mochica

Such lifelike ceramics are to be found nowhere else again except in the civilization of Moche, on the north coast of Peru. To the group scenes (Ill. 35) like those from Colima on the northwest coast of Mexico, there is a parallel thousands of miles further south. In neither region was anything considered of too little importance or too frivolous to be given as a lifelike and lively offering to the dead. We witness a naive and original force: scenes of festivity—some of the celebrants dancing joyfully, others drunk on too much maize beer, the forbidden fifth beaker. Models of houses have been found in shaft-graves of northwest Mexico and in the coastal cemeteries of Peru, long outliving the actual houses themselves (Ill. 40, 103). In Peru, one is struck by yet another parallel to the Colima civilization. These two civilizations are unique in the pre-Columbian era in that their art shows no trace of a chastity taboo. With the representation and the exaggeration of the genitals, the ceramics of the northwest coast seem alien to early Mexican art. At least after the classic period, Mexican artists always avoided showing the naked body and tended to obliterate the differences between man and woman, so that, in many cases, it is difficult to say whether the image is that of a priestess or of a dignitary. The Mochicas, unique among the civilizations of ancient Peru, went even further with their immensely naturalistic ceramics. In the works of these talented sculptors, not even the most intimate subjects are excluded but are found represented in great numbers. They are among the oldest testimonies to eroticism (Ill. 104, 110b, 111).

Not one authentic written source leads back to the civilization of Moche; only extensive records in clay, the offerings in the graves showing scenery in great detail, open their world to us.

There is, however, no lack of interpretation of these tacit but eloquent witnesses from the world of the dead. The Mochicas are somewhat of a curiosity for the interpreter—they are the only race in the central Andes who emphasize sexuality to any great extent—no other people attaches so much importance to the sexual instinct.

The Peruvian archaeologist, R. Larco Hoyle[12] (1965), believes he can see in the very realistic representations of coitus that the woman did not share the sexual passion of the man. On the contrary, he thinks that the features of the women disclose in many cases reluctance, even disgust; the talent of the sculptors shows all shades of emotion: pain or satisfaction, tears as well as laughter. Here virility is emphasized while woman is relegated to the background. She evidently was deemed fit only to bear children, to care for them and to work in the fields, a view later shared by the Spanish chroniclers. We meet her only as the servant of man's sexual desire, while the man takes up a striking attitude as warrior, hunter or fisherman; his sexual activity points to his warlike and dominating nature. By contrast, the woman was suppressed and ruled by her male partner.

It may be observed that these ceramics have raised a monument to man and lost sight of woman. Yet a certain amount of criticism of the man's attitude is not missing in the ceramics, notwithstanding the exhibited manliness of the male. In the several thousand images of women which have been found, the woman nearly always looks fresh and modest. For her, coitus is a natural act in which she sees nothing blameworthy. It is different with the man, who already shows the marks of vice in his face. Innumerable folds and wrinkles, frequently even a head like a skull, are evidently the price of uninhibited sexual activity.

A different interpretation was advanced in 1925 by Posnansky,[13] who believed that he recognized in the sculptures a psychopathic constitution in the artists.

Besides the explicitly erotic sculptures and the realistic scenes of everyday life, there are representations of religious subjects: the jaguar, the felid, standing on its hind legs, rapes or fertilizes a woman, the symbol of growth (Ill. 107). In some of the decorations of vessels and of ornaments in woven fabrics, this wild-cat goddess appears as a religious symbol, with a phallus shaped like a wide-branching tree or a root. In both these cases, this symbolizes the fertilizing power of the realm of nature. In the last period of the Mochica civilization the jaguar is shown in a fully human form; but the wrinkled face, exaggerated eyebrows and whiskers, and the strikingly large eye-teeth point to its ancestor. It may be assumed that the priests tried to identify themselves, with the help of masks and garments, with their prototype from nature. As many items of this ceramic art are of a sacred nature, Feriz[14] (1959) sees in the "immovable and serious, often solemn" expressions of the couples during coition an indication of the religious importance of this act.

Because of these divergent explanations, it seems wise to refrain from interpretations. This applies equally to the assumption by Victor von Hagen[15] (1965) that only women, owing to their appreciation of sex, were able to produce these and also other equally expressive ceramics in old Peru. The different opinions held by these four archaeologists, based solely on the material found in the graves, shows how scanty our knowledge of Peru is up to the period of about seventy years before the conquest.

The civilizations of Tlatilco, Colima, and Mochica are those in which we find the material that most enriches our limited knowledge of woman in pre-classical times (that is, before the twelfth century). They are more rewarding in this respect than the classical theocratic high civilizations which fail to depict woman except as goddess or priestess. The custom of making erotic offerings to the dead disappeared when the Huari culture spread all over Peru—we are thus deprived of a potential source of information about the sexual life of woman in old America. Some insight into the subject is gained, however, from traditional legends and from such portions of ancient law as the Spaniards thought worth recording. Although the Spaniards landing on the north coast met among the chiefs some female ones, yet men seem to have played the dominant role in religion and social life in the pre-Columbian civilizations of Peru.

THE AZTEC WOMAN

In ancient America, the life of the woman of the lower strata of society was, even more than that of the man, largely determined by her birth. Her mind was formed by her severe upbringing. Unless she became a refugee, or wars or exceptional natural catastrophes descended upon her, her life went by evenly and monotonously, as did the lives of the other members of the tribe.

In public life the woman was not much in view. Her activities were relegated to home and family life. Priestesses, dancers, and courtesans as well as the wives of the rulers formed exceptions; we shall mention them later on.

From reliable Aztec sources, it is possible to follow the life of an Aztec girl from birth to marriage.

Pregnancy and Childbirth

The pregnant woman of the Aztecs was protected by at least three to four goddesses, among them Teteoinnan, the birth goddess and earth goddess, the patron saint of the midwives, who had a similar social rank as had the professional matchmakers or the lay priestesses. Supplicated most frequently on behalf of the mother-to-be was Ayopechcatl, the "One having her realm in the mist," the small goddess of confinement.

"Down there in the house of Ayopechcatl a jewel has
   been born, a child has come into the world.
   Down there, with her, children are born.
   Come, come on, you newcomer, come on!
   Come, come on, jewel-child, come on!"

With these magical prayers, their words repeated as an incantation, the patient adapted herself to the new situation. The roots of many of these archaic prayers are to be found in shamanism and seem to go back to earlier concepts.

According to the Aztecs' ideas, every being, and also the unborn child, was exposed to irrational and magical powers. A kind of primitive fear took hold of the Aztec woman the moment she knew herself to be pregnant. Quite a number of precautionary measures and taboos had to be observed: should she see any red objects, the child would be born the wrong way round. Going out at night she had to sprinkle ashes under her blouse to prevent her being terrified by ghosts. If she looked at the sky during an eclipse of the sun, the child would be born with a hare-lip, unless she wore a knife of obsidian on her bare skin under her clothes. The exposure to suffering right from the beginning made the Indian women invulnerable, imperturbable, insensitive.

"Listen, all you who are present here,
all, as you are assembled here . . .
Yoalliehecatl, the 'wind at night,'
has shown mercy to us,
as he has put into the young woman,
into the recently married one, a jewel,
a quetzal-feather.
She, the young woman, is pregnant.
He, our lord,
has put a child into her."

Words like these, announcing the event in the family circle, were followed by numerous speeches from parents and relatives. In all such prayers expression was given to the ever present thought of death. The transitoriness of all life, the reflection that the new-born could pass away as quickly as it had been begotten, this was the quintessence of these flowery speeches.

The midwife (ciuatl temixiuitl) was consulted as early as in the first months of pregnancy. She accompanied the pregnant woman to a hot bath, protected by the goddess Tlazoltéotl, and massaged her after the bath. The bath had to be not too hot, so that the child should not "stick on." Moreover, the expectant mother was not allowed to fast, but had to eat well-cooked food. She was not to work hard or lift heavy weights. Every shock had to be avoided, so that there should be no miscarriage. Fire and sun were not to heat her body overmuch. The midwife further advised the woman to continue in a moderate way to cohabit with her husband for three months after the beginning of the pregnancy, as complete abstinence was believed to deprive the child of strength.

In the days immediately before the birth the help of the midwife became more intense. When labor pains developed, she gave medicines to hasten the process; drinks of pounded Peruvian bark (chinin) and healing herbs, later a piece of the finely chopped tail of an oppussum (tlaquatzín). This concoction was supposed to have an immediate effect.

At the moment of the birth the midwife emitted a war cry, as the woman giving birth was honoured by the Aztecs like a warrior who has taken a prisoner. The helper cut the umbilical cord and buried it in a corner of the house. Praying in a low voice to the water goddess Chalchiuhtlicue ("the Lady with the skirt of jade"), she washed the child. While doing so, she "softly blew

breath into the water" (she breathed into it), then gave a drop of it to the new-born and later wetted its chest, neck and head. Finally the child was dipped into the water, dried and swathed.

The Mexicans especially were very fond of children, but their pleasure could be somewhat less intense, particularly at a first birth, if the child was a girl. If, however, it was a boy, the midwife said to him: "You are a quecholli bird; the house in which you see the light is only a nest," and she continued by pointing already to his duties: "You are destined to refresh the sun with the blood of your enemies and to feed the earth Tlaltecuhtli with their bodies. Your fatherland, your heir, your father belong to the realm of the sun, they belong to heaven."[16]

Girls were greeted with other words: "You must be in the house like the heart in the body. You must not leave the house . . . You must be like the ashes and the hearth." While the man was from the first minute of his life chained to the lot of the warrior, the woman was obligated to house and family. The male infant was shown weapons, while to the newborn daughter the mother showed wool and a spindle.

Only then followed the greetings of welcome from the midwife, which have been transmitted to us by Sahagún, showing that she was not only an assistant in childbirth but also a lay priestess. These greetings clearly reveal the Aztec attitude toward life; we, therefore, reproduce them in full. It is the greeting of welcome to a traveller, for man is supposed to be a traveller coming from one of the upper or under-worlds so as to continue wandering in yet another world. According to the conception of the ancient Mexicans, life was only a temporary transit station.

"You have now come into the world where your parents live amidst cares and toil, where glowing heat, cold and winds prevail, where there is neither real joy nor satisfaction, for it is a place of work, cares and want. My daughter, we do not know whether you will live long enough on earth to know your grandparents, nor whether they will some day be able to rejoice about you. We do not know what fate is prepared for you, nor which are the gifts and the mercies which are given to you by your Father and your Mother, the great Master and the great Mistress who reside in heaven. We do not know what you are bringing to us, nor what will be your fate, whether you bring something that gives us pleasure. We do not know whether you will unfold, whether He, through whom we live, will let you grow and ripen. We do not know whether you have good qualities, whether you perhaps are born as an empty cob of corn which is of no value; whether you bring with you bad predispositions, whether you will expose yourself to dirt and vice or whether you will turn out a rogue. What is it with which you are blessed? What is it that you have been given like a thing that one binds in a cloth ere the sun shines?

"Be welcome, my daughter, we rejoice at your coming, you our beloved are our precious stone, our quetzal-feather, our lovely thing. You have arrived, now rest from your weariness: here we are, your relatives, waiting for you. You have been put into their hands under their care.

"You must not sigh, not weep to have come. Your arrival has been longed for. Yet there will be work and toil for you, because this is the wish of our Master and his decision that we shall obtain all that is needed for life only through sweat, only through work . . .

"My daughter, if you remain alive, you will see this for yourself. You are very welcome, very welcome are you.

"He who is omnipresent,
Who is your Father and your Mother,
The Father of all,
May He protect you.
May He adorn you, may He care for you.

"Although you are our daughter, we do not deserve to have you. Small as you are, He can call you, He who created you. Then you will be like something which passes before our eyes; we see you for one moment and then never more. Beloved child, let us set our hope in our Master."

Most Spaniards compared the ablutions with baptism. The concept of original sin, too, led several chroniclers to assume that the Aztecs had Christian notions. But all this had nothing to do with Christianity. The Indians fought right from the beginning against imaginary beings—against the demons of their imagination, relics of the past, ghosts which they had themselves introduced into the world. These demons had become for them real beings, and their reality was subtle, cruel, deceitful. They were intangible, unconquerable, especially as they lived not outside but in the thoughts of men themselves. They personified the unexpected, the absolute in disappointment. The permanent fight against them, supported by the will to live, and by hope—all this had a strong antagonist: the fear of nonexistence. This fear induced the Aztecs to expect the end of the world every fifty-two years at the end of a "bundle of years." Then all fires were extinguished, all furniture destroyed and the next day's rising sun anxiously awaited.

The woman who died in childbirth deserved the same honours as the warrior fallen in battle. An equal heaven awaited them, an equally honourable task. The fallen warriors accompanied the sun god Tonatiuh from the house of the god in the eastern sky to the zenith, with songs and dances, and then, disguised as precious birds and butterflies, fluttered down to the earth to refresh themselves with honey and the juice of blossoms; similarly the souls of the "warriors in female shape" (moci-uaquetzque), the women who died in childbirth, met the sun in the zenith and accompanied it to its setting in the western sky. The living, however, were afraid of them, because they were no friendly ghosts, like the male warriors, but night ghosts (tzitzimime) which lay in wait at crossroads, wished epilepsy on children and incited men to lewdness.

Horoscopes: The Book of Days

If the outcome of the confinement was a happy one for mother and child, it became the first care of the parents to find out whether the child was born under favourable auspices. A tonalpouhqui, or fortune-teller, who was conversant with the meanings and the interpretation of the tonalamatl, the "Book of Days," was therefore called to the house as soon as possible. In return for his services he was given cloth, turkeys and a share in the baptismal meal. To begin with he enquired as to the exact time of the birth and then he set the horoscope. If the time of birth was favourable, he announced: "Your child is born under favourable auspices." But his verdict could be just as well: "The child is born under unfavourable auspices, yet there is in the same row a more acceptable sign which weakens and counterbalances the destructive influence of the main sign." It was as a rule possible to choose a better date, however. The Mexican calendar was composed of twenty diverse symbols and thirteen numbers connected with them, and the signs with the number seven were always favourable. Other numbers too were able to reduce the influence of the unfavourable symbols; moreover, one could seek safety by postponing the baptism for four days. Cipactli, the day-hiero-

glyph for "crocodile," was for girls a decidedly "favour-able star." They could expect no lack of worldly goods, and all that they started was bound to succeed. If a girl's day symbol was flower *(xochitl)*, she was to turn out, according to the horoscope, a good weaver, a good housewife, but could equally well, if she neglected the prayer exercises, become a prostitute, because the ambiguity of this symbol is explained in connection with the goddess of vegetation Xochiquetzal (Precious Flower), who was the protector of female handicrafts and simultaneously the goddess of lustfulness.

If the infant girl was born under the symbol "movement" *(olin)*, she developed into an excitingly beautiful woman. All she undertook quickly accelerated to the pitch of frenzy. Born under this symbol, the girl could not be bound. Nevertheless, if after a long search she had found the right partner, she became faithful and a good housewife.

Those born under the "jaguar" *(ocelotl)* sign had to expect a life full of toil. According to their horoscope, "jaguar-women" were destined to be adulteresses. The "rabbit-ladies" tended to drunkenness and the "eagle-

women" were shrewish like Xanthippes. It was unpleasant for women to have first seen the light on the day "reed" *(acatl)*, because it was prophesied to them that they would be stupid, loquacious, arrogant and slanderous. As the prophecies in the calendar further showed them to be also lazy and of no use for any work, the family sometimes tried to sell them as slaves, who later, on special religious occasions, would be sacrificed. This would confirm my opinion that the excessive human sacrifices of the Aztecs are to be attributed mainly to overpopulation in the high valleys, since both sacrifices of prisoners and of slaves had been comparatively rare in the pre-Aztec time. There was apparently, along with the religious duty to feed and to strengthen the gods with the most precious human possession, human blood, also the economic duty to get rid of superfluous mouths.

In the case of a large number of bad omens it proved necessary to enlist the scholars of the calendar-science and fortune-tellers, as they alone were able to reduce the destined importance of the symbols by combining them with certain numbers. They could even change the prophecies to their opposites by replacing in their calcu-

20

lations the number of the day of birth by that which they chose for the baptism. Of course, the good prophecies could come true only if the woman led a modest life and regularly did penance. The fortune-teller had made himself safe in any case; he had made in good time a cover of "ifs" and "buts."

While the sun year *(xihuitl)* had 360 days plus 5 "superfluous" days, the years of the fortune-tellers' calendar consisted, and that was important for it, of only 260 days. It began with I *cipactli* or I "crocodile" and ended with 13 *xochitl* or 13 "flower." So the chronology of the sun year and of the fortune-tellers' calendar went side by side. The arrangement of the system was so clear that every day could be seen in both calendars without much difficulty.

Important for the fortune-teller were also the gods who were allotted in regular cycles to the symbols of the day: sun and moon deities to I *miquitztli* (I death); Petécatl, the god of drunkenness, to I *cuauhtli* (I eagle) to mention only a few. The fortune-teller, of course, made use of these gods when he tried to discover the nature of what was to happen. Of similar importance were the ascendants, the deities of the four points of the compass: the special qualities of the east are fertility and plenty, those of the north raw climate and drought, of the west old age and death, of the south abundance and uncertainty. The geographical situation of the country, with its different climatic zones, is responsible for this conception.

The life of the Mexicans was of course determined and regulated to a large extent by these prophecies of the *tonalamatl*. The merchants, for instance, waited for certain days to start on their hazardous journeys through territories of foreign tribes, although it was precisely the members of this occupation who had a kind of safe-conduct passport in ancient Mexico. "One jaguar" was the day on which prisoners of war and female slaves were sacrificed. The day for marriage, too, was fixed after calculation. One can safely assume that no Aztec of whatever descent or rank could have dispensed with the prophecies of the fortune-teller.

To give an indication of the tremendous importance of the calendar for everybody from the least subject to the ruler Moctezuma II, it may be mentioned that a sequence of unhappy omens, which preceded the Spanish conquest, paralyzed the Aztecs' determination to resist the invaders.

This philosophy allowed Mexican man but little freedom of action; he was ruled by the Damocles' sword of his predestination. He was ensnared by the day symbol of his birth with uncanny, unreal powers. The weight of the gods and the stars crushed him. The omnipotence of the calendar and concepts connected with it made him a slave. So, his thinking was interwoven with his fatalism, yet it was an active one. He fought with cunning against fate and his predestination: perhaps he postponed the baptism of his child for four days, hoping thereby to gain a better day-symbol, or perhaps only because, as a Mexican, he refused to give in to the prophecy. On the one hand, he was prepared to accept the world only as a transit station; on the other, he was determined to fight tirelessly against the questionable existence that the gods tried to fix upon him.

Education

When the "Mexica" had ended their restless nomadic existence and in the course of some few generations had assimilated into the long-established tribes, the social structure was fundamentally changed. One of the most important achievements was the introduction of compulsory education. The date when this was done cannot be ascertained exactly; that it happened was a tremendous achievement for that time. In the Middle Ages, when in Europe school education was a privilege of the upper classes, there was in the Aztec society not a single child, of whatever origin, who grew up without it. The state took care of the education of children. With immense solicitude it tried to further civilization, to uphold morals, and to train useful subjects.

At the age of twelve, the young Aztecs were given the full ration of two maize cakes. At the age of fifteen (according to the *Codex Mendoza;* other sources mention an earlier age), the parents entrusted their children to the public schools, where they would live until they were of marriageable age. For the boys, the teaching in the "House of Youth" *(telpochcalli)* consisted chiefly of instruction in civic duties and in the use of arms; while the young girls learned to weave and also to make very precious embroidered feather cloaks. The curriculum included knowledge of the history and traditions of the tribe and of the religious and lay rites.

The boys were also employed in some of the less splendid labours, such as the cleaning of canals and streets;

Education of a young girl (Codex Mendoza)

they found their reward after sunset in the *cuicacalco*, the "House of Song." A chronicler says, "here the young people danced until after midnight. He who had a girl friend slept with her." The young men shared this common life not with girls who also had to go to school, but with the *auianime*, the prostitutes. This arrangement was permitted by the school authorities.

This kind of free school might seem somewhat strange to us. Sahagún was the first European who spoke deprecatingly of the young people in the *telpochcalli*: "They do not lead a decent life, for they entertain prostitutes, speak frivolously and cynically, and show themselves arrogant and proud."

He sympathized most with the pupils in the *calmecac*, a kind of monastery school, where the members of the clergy were trained. There the boys and girls were taught everything that formed part of the contemporary knowledge of that country: writing and the interpretation of the pictographs, prophecy and the rules of the calendar, poetry and the high art of oratory. If the parents decided for the *calmecac*, the little girls were registered there soon after their birth, and, between the fourth and sixth year of age, handed over to the school. Later, they were free to choose whether they wanted to leave or to devote their lives to the service of religion.

Although this educational system reflects the different social classes of Aztec society, there were also for young people of lowly origin no insuperable barriers. Even the sons of plebeians were admitted to this élite school, depending on their intelligence and their parents' desires. Pupils could also change over from one school to another. With such an education, even pupils of the "people's college" could in theory aim at the post of a *tlacochcalcatl*, of the highest war-lord. It is, however, not known whether a man of lowly descent ever really obtained such a post.

Marriage

When the boys and girls had reached marriageable age, they left school. Courtship was always initiated by the young man's family. The family solicited the help of matrimonial agents, who were eloquent and conversant with the rites. As the young men and young girls had not been brought up in the house of their parents, a petition had first to be submitted to the teacher (*telpochtlatoque*, the "director of the young men"). If then the director of the school came at the father's request to his house, it was usual to entertain him and to make him presents. After the meal, the relatives of the twenty-year old pupil sat down together in a circle and put down a copper axe in front of the *telpochtlatoque*.

"Relatives and teacher, do not be sad because your brother, our son, will separate himself from you. He wants to take a wife. Look at this axe here: it is a symbol that he does want to separate himself from your community. Take it and discharge our son." The teacher replied with solemn words to the speech of the father and discharged the boy from the school. Then only was it possible to look for a wife for him. This, too, was the duty of the family and of the council of elders.

"The father is the root and the base of the family;" so reads a passage in one of the texts on ancient Mexico which Sahagún has copied. This patriarchal conception determined nearly all steps which the young people had to take. Thus, the marriage, the birth of children and the choice of names for them were not the affair of an individual but that of the family council which was presided over by the father. As with the Incas, the marriage was a demand of the society one had to fulfil towards ones parents and the state. The young people may have been permitted to make requests to their parents; this seems to have been easier for men, while for girls the free choice of a husband was nearly impossible.

After the consultations, the matrimonial agent was asked to go to the house of the chosen girl to request the consent of her parents. Of course, this ceremony could not end without a flowery speech, and invariably the parents of the young girl at first refused eloquently. The reasons were enumerated very politely in detail: the daughter was still too young, she had not enough experience and was simply unworthy of such a splendid husband. But this refusal did not mean anything. It was a fixed part of the wooing, which lasted for several days. Then the matrimonial agent was spoken to as follows:

"Dear woman, you are taking great trouble on behalf of this girl, whom you require so urgently as wife for this young man. We cannot understand how he could be so mistaken as to want only her as a wife, for she is good for nothing, still a stupid thing. But as you urge us, we must first hear what our aunts and uncles, the male and the female relatives, think about it. Therefore come back tomorrow and you shall be given a definite answer."

It was characteristic that the daughter had to listen to what the other members of the family had to say. She herself was not entitled to say anything in what concerned herself. Humiliation, even in the circle of her relatives, never any praise, formed part of the polite ceremonial. The following words had to be uttered in the house of the girl's parents before one could notice the first breath of sympathy: "... and although our daughter does not understand anything and is inexperienced in all female duties, it seems to us that the young man is fond of her." Notwithstanding the painstaking detail and the love of long-winded phrases in the writings of Sahagún and his informants, we still do not know whether a dowry was required from the bride or whether the young man had to bring presents for the bride. (We know of the Maya Indians that the man had to work from four to six years in the house of his parents-in-law.)

Friends and relatives of both families could be invited, and the festivities could be started, only after the priests, who had inquired as to the horoscope at the birth, had chosen in the "Book of Days" a propitious day: that is a day under the calendar symbol *acatl* (reed), *ozomatli* (monkey) or *cuauhtli* (eagle).

On her wedding day the bride was bathed, her hair washed, her face made up with ochre and powdered with sulphur pyrites shimmering like gold. Feathers of exotic birds were stuck on her arms and she was, of course, dressed in her most richly embroidered and most beautiful garment.

The old people warned her that she now no longer was a young girl and was not to behave like a child. From now on she had to get up at night, sweep the house and light the fire before daybreak. "Make us not ashamed, we who are your relatives, don't bring shame on your fathers and mothers." These or similar words were an admonition on the part of her parents.

At sunset the bridegroom's family came to the house of the bride. Entering, they apologized with the customary words: "We hope we are no nuisance with our trampling. Please understand, we have come to fetch our daughter. We want to take her with us." Then an old woman spread a black cloth *(tlilquemitl)* on which the bride knelt down. The old woman gathered the corners together and in this large wrap *(rebozo)* she lifted the young woman on her back. Other women lit torches—as shown by an illustration of the *Codex Mendoza*—and the procession of the women started solemnly.

In the streets the curious neighbours greeted the bride's procession with acclamations and exhortations. Nor did her parents cease giving advice and solemn admonitions.

In the house of the man's parents, the bride was set down on a straw mat beside the hearth. The bridegroom sat at her right on the mat. As a symbolic act, the matrimonial agent knotted the corners of the man's wrap together with the bride's shirt. Then she took some maize cake from a plate and gave four bites of it to each of them. Thus, the marriage had taken place. The "priestess of matrimony" then led the newly wedded into a room and left them alone. All through the night she stood guard at the door.

The festivities were said to have lasted four days, and it is likely that the fifth beaker of pulque was emptied by the guests. Only on the fourth day (for until then every night one of the women had stood guard before the door of the newly wed) could the matrimonial agent end the ceremonies by taking the young couple's mat and shaking it out in the courtyard. It would not have been an Aztec ending had there been no speeches and return speeches. The female relatives of the man said to the bride: "My daughter, be strong and do not grieve because of the burden of marriage which you have to bear; pray to the gods that they help you to ascend the hill of work. Perhaps you will reach the summit without difficulties, without getting tired. Here are five cloths which your husband gives you, to get in exchange for them in the market the things you need to prepare the food: chili pepper, firewood, salt and other things. This is ordered by the customs we have received from the ancients. Mark, my daughter, you must yourself look after your domestic duties, no one will help you."

Quite different sentiments came from the young man's mother-in-law. "Here you are standing before me, my son, our jaguar, our eagle, our quetzal-feather, our jewel. Now you are our tenderly beloved son. Understand that you are a married man, that our daughter is your wife. This does not seem a trifle to us, and it is another world from which you now speak to us. Of course you must now as a man adopt other habits than those you have had before now. You are a man and have not any more the soul of a boy. It is no longer seemly for you to be like a high-spirited youth and to take part in the entertainments and pleasures of the bachelors, or in buffoonery, and, most of all, you must not go to the brothels; for you are a married man."

Social Organization

Through matrimony the Aztec woman exchanged bondage to her father for bondage to her husband.

She was taken into the *calpulli* ("big house") of her husband. If she was already a widow with children, she usually married the brother of her husband, who in any case had to act as a father to the children. Only the sons or the father's brother had a claim to the inheritance, not the daughters, as otherwise the patriarchal relationship to the *calpulli* could not have been sustained. To explain this, it is necessary to have a look at the social organization in the period of the Aztecs' rule.

At the time of their immigration into the high valley of Mexico the social organization of the Aztecs still hardly differed from that of the other nomads on the continent. According to the legends, there were seven (in other traditions, ten) originally probably totemistic clans, which, under the guidance of their chiefs, entered the

fertile high valley around 1300. Superior to these chiefs were the four "house masters" *(huitzilopochtli)*. After the foundation of Tenochtitlán (at present the capital of Mexico) by Tenoch, the clans were organized in twenty local groups, where, inside the four big districts in the town, members formed their own settlements.

It cannot any longer be ascertained whether each of these *calpulli* was formed by the union of five clans; but it is certain that the members of a *calpulli* had to seek marriage partners in one of the other "big houses," upholding in this way an ancient law against incest. Among the Aztecs marriages between blood relatives, step-parents and step-children, parents-in-law and children-in-law were most severely punished, while among the Mixtecs, the neighbouring tribe to the south, marriages between brothers and sisters were usual, at least for the nobility.

In this civilization, definitely ruled by men, woman was not equal to man. Premarital virginity and absolute faithfulness when married were peremptorily demanded

of her; there were no laws like these for the man. Unfaithfulness was by law to be punished by stoning. The same punishment threatened the husband, but evidently only "on paper."

Divorce was possible only with the consent of a judge. The request was, however, not made directly for divorce but for permission to the plaintiff to do what he thought to be right. In this way the judge could allow the divorce without saying so outright.

The grounds for which a man could obtain a divorce were liberal. The husband could ask for it if the wife proved herself to be quarrelsome, impatient, careless or inefficient. Divorce was granted for proved faults of character without any need to prove an attitude inimical to the marriage. Barrenness was the outstanding reason for divorce.[17] In special cases the wife, too, was entitled to ask for divorce, but the relevant passages of the law of Nezahualcoyotl[18] have been lost.

The chattels of the husband and wife remained separate. Lists were made of what was brought to the marriage, so that in case of divorce one would know what belonged to each partner.

The sons of the divorced were allocated to the father, the daughters to the mother. Capital punishment was stipulated for divorced persons if they remarried one another. Marriage was also forbidden between relatives and in-laws in direct line, and between brother and sister. These laws also applied to the royal family. Further, it was forbidden to marry the father's concubine, while marriage with the daughter of the mother's brother was permitted. In the ruling families it was lawful to take the cousin as concubine. The prohibition against marrying the stepmother was not strictly observed in all parts of Mexico. In Michoacán a man had to marry, along with a woman, her daughter from a previous marriage, that is, in other words, with the daughter the mother also; the Aztecs, however, did not approve of this.

Marriage was governed by patriarchal law. The father had authority over the child; the father's heir was his son, and the father was entitled to decide upon the marriage of the child. But the mother could influence these decisions.

In time of need, the parents could sell their children as slaves; the sale was legally approved and documented. According to law, there were no born slaves. The child born by a slave entered the world as a free individual. It frequently happened, however, that, when everything else had been lost in gambling, the children's freedom was staked and they became slaves. The parents further had the right to condemn an incorrigible son to slavery.[19] Opinions vary as to whether a man who associated with the female slave of another was liable to be made the slave of her master. According to reliable sources, such an enslavement took place only as compensation for the injury to the slave herself, especially if she died at her confinement. The sacrifice of slaves at funerals was frequently practised in order that the slave might continue to be a servant in the other life. By marrying the master or the mistress a slave gained her or his freedom.

THE MAYAS AND THEIR SOUTHERN NEIGHBORS

South from Mexico in Guatemala, in eastern Honduras and northern Salvador, in the home of the Maya Indians, the volume of evidence of a great past increases while the written sources of the early colonists dry up. The main reason for this is the fact that in this territory where large states never developed, the Spaniards met with strong opposition. The country was completely conquered only in 1697, almost two hundred years after the first conquistadores had landed.

The nation of the Mayas, based on a common language and race, formed only in the classical period a cultural and ideological unity, but was rent by quarrels and fighting during long epochs. The people lived in family groups in fixed localities and joined together to form larger clans. The Quiché Mayas in the highlands of Guatemala called the union of three clans *nimha*.

The most important ceremony in the life of the Mayas, for the girls as well as for the boys, was the "second birth" (*caput zihil*) through which they were officially admitted to the clan. It consisted chiefly in a ceremonial cleansing of the children, sacrificial gifts for the gods, a confession and a religious ablution.

For girls the number three was of great importance, three being the sacred number for the woman. Three stones formed the border of the hearth, where as a woman she would spend most of her life. A boy's fourth month of life was the occasion of a festivity, as this was his sacred number, which corresponded to the four sides of the field of maize.

When the girl reached the age of sixty days (the Mayas' months consisted of twenty days), the mother took her in her arms and handed her over to the wife of the *kazike*, or chief. This was done in the middle of the hut. On a straw mat lay a spindle, cotton, a miniature weaver's loom, needles made of bones and the thorns of cactuses, a small water-jug, a cooking-pot, and the *metate*, the millstone for maize.

"Take this so that you may learn to spin the cotton," said the mother and gave some of the cotton to the infant. Then the baby was carried nine times around the mat. The adults took the miniature loom and made the movements of weaving. With these ceremonies the infant girl was introduced to the community as one of its members.

As far as we know, there was for girls no education in the public schools as practised, for instance, in Tenochtitlán, the capital of the Aztecs.

Marriage

The organization of the clans was of the greatest importance for marriage. Looking back, one discovers in the earliest times the surviving vestiges of an ancient matriarchy, while all later periods tend towards establishing the succession of the father. Only in the arid peninsula of Yucatán was the name of the mother's clan still given first place, before that of the father's, until even shortly before the Spanish conquest.

The role of the incest taboo is nowhere in any of the old American civilizations so difficult to understand as in the case of the ancient Mayas. There are linguistic proofs of the existence of an ancient system of marriages of cousins according to which the man married the daughter of his father's sister; but the word "sister" might have been used in a wider sense than nowadays. For example, Diego de Landa reports from Yucatán the prohibition of marriage for members of the father's family bearing the same name, while the marriage of cousins in the mother's family was permitted.[20] Although our knowledge of the system of totemistic clans is incomplete, it is certain that marriage of persons with the same totem-animal was forbidden. The prohibition of the marriage of persons with the same name, which we know to have existed in Yucatán, may have been a remnant of this ancient clan organization; this had, however, largely broken down when the Spaniards landed. Only in some remote regions of the highlands of Chiapas and of Guatemala did the Europeans on their arrival find the clan organization still intact, with marriages permitted only outside the clan.

In the peninsula of Yucatán the young men lived in "men's houses" until they were married. At the age of twenty, they could venture to look at the young girls from the village, and to make their choice among those daily fetching water from the well, or those whom they met by chance at the market. The young man discussed this with his father, because the mother seems to have left this completely to him. If the father approved, he dealt also with the matrimonial agent, who had to pay frequent visits to the girl's parents. Contrary to Aztec custom, the Mayas were apt to describe eloquently the beauty and the domestic virtues of their child. The "young flower," the "quetzal-feather," or the "precious stone"—these were the usual names of the young girls—was the best of all weavers, her *tamales* (little rolls of maize with savoury filling) were known all over the district, and by the sway of her hips one could already see what outstanding children she would bear. The girl praised in this way could hope for an early marriage if her parents entertained the agent of the young man with a drink of cocoa and chili pepper. For a family of modest means it was a costly drink, a drink in fact reserved for the nobility, as cocoa was not grown in Yucatán, but came from another region. Accordingly, the goods to be exchanged for it were very valuable. At the end of this pleasant part of the evening, the matrimonial agent suggested an alliance of the two families through the marriage of the young couple. Then began the haggling about the price. It was true haggling, and the parents of the girl were in no hurry. It was, so they said, not necessary to ask for such a large bride price on the grounds that the girl was particularly outstanding, but only because it was the custom. When the matter of the "presents"—cotton, tobacco, copal, cocoa beans and so on—had been settled, there arose the question of the number of years the young son-in-law would have to work after the wedding in the house of the bride's parents. For the family of the young man this arrangement was costly, as they lost an efficient and indispensable worker. Service to the father-in-law lasted from four to six years. Only after this could the young man think of setting up his own household, and working his own field; a Maya wife, even from the lowest ranks, was not cheap.

The bargain concluded, the matrimonial agent consulted the priest, who usually was also the chief of the settlement. He declared that the two persons had not the same name from the paternal family, therefore were not blood relatives, and that there had not been any serious conflicts between the gods on whose days the young people had been born. As with the Aztecs, the day on which anyone was born played a large, fateful role. As the result of these studies of the birthdays, paid for with a load of maize, the priest suggested a few favourable days for the wedding. Usually it took place on the day of the moon goddess *(I caban)* who was the protector of matrimony and motherhood.

The blouse *(kub)* and the wedding-skirt *(pic)* made for the young girl had to be ready by the time of the wedding. Then the parents informed relatives and friends. This, however, was done not quite altruistically: enjoying quantities of pulque, an alcoholic drink made of the fermented juice of the agave, the family and their friends started together to build a house for the young couple. The hut, made of wooden posts, branches and palm leaves, was built in two days. Other friends provided large quantities of game and turkeys, which, apart from dogs, were the only domestic animals in those parts. The women prepared a bean porridge, sweet potatoes and the *tortillas* of maize.

This was a cheap way for the young couple to acquire a home; in Indian communities it was taken as a matter of course that one helped one's neighbor; one would come to the rescue in the same way whenever his neighbor was in a similar situation.

The household goods of the young couple were simple. They consisted of the millstone *(metate)*, a few cooking pots, earthen pans, jugs for storage, baskets, bottle-gourds for the kitchen, straw-mats *(petate)* or hammocks, and a few covers made of bark; these were the objects most necessary for everyday life.

When all this was assembled, the festivities began. For the guests a true Indian festivity consisted of a plentiful feast of tasty food and alcoholic drinks. Nor was there any lack of flowery speeches.

The difference between the rather Dionysian inhabitants of the lowlands and the more ascetic and contemplative people of the highlands, like the Aztecs, is evident in the exhortations given to the young couple. They were less strict, and the prospects for the future were viewed with less pessimism than among the Aztecs.

The chief, acting in Yucatán and Nicaragua also as priest, showed the young couple into their hut, holding them all the time by the little finger of their left hand. He addressed admonitory words to them, lit some copal resin in a small bowl and kindled the wood in the hearth. After a short sermon to the young couple, who sat facing each other on a mat, he left them alone. Without moving and without exchanging a word, they looked into the fire until it went out: this formed part of the ceremony. "Then they are married and so carry on," reported the Spanish chronicler Oviedo.[21] For the guests staying in the house of the bride's parents, the festivities reached their climax that night.

The next morning, as early as one hour before sunrise, the young wife left her husband's hammock, lit the fire and started making breakfast. At sunrise she awoke her husband and shared the breakfast with him. There was no honeymoon in the life of the Indian; the man went hunting or to his work in the fields. The next event of

importance for the young couple, and especially of course for the wife, was pregnancy, since childlessness was one of the main reasons for divorce.

Apart from childlessness, there was another ground on which the man was entitled to reject his wife immediately after the first night, and to ask for his marriage portion to be returned: that is, if at marriage the bride was no longer a virgin. It was, however, said of the majority of the young men that they preferred an experienced girl, as in Peru, where virginity was of little importance. But the ancient reports are contradictory. Some mention that virginity was deemed necessary among the Mayas, as among the Aztecs. According to the chronicler the reason for the two-fold interpretation is to be found in the fact "that one asks the father or the mother of the bride whether she is still a virgin. If parents answer in the affirmative, and the husband then discovers the contrary to be the case, he gives her back to her parents and thereby regains his freedom. The girl is then considered to fall into disrepute. But if, although she is no longer a virgin, an agreement is reached with regard to this, then the wedding takes place after all, as many men prefer a deflowered girl to a virgin."[22] The husband therefore complained not so much about the fact itself but about the abuse of his trust. What happened here on a small scale was an abuse multiplied a thousand-fold by the Spaniards in their conquests. The Indians were constantly outwitted with lies, since, owing to their education and way of life, they were unable to deal with them. The abuse of trust within the family, or a similar offence against the state, was thought to be the most heinous of crimes.

According to reliable accounts, divorce by mutual consent, that is, divorce not due to an abuse of trust, was quite common in Yucatán; this is the region concerning which there is the largest number of reliable sources. Each member of a divorced couple could marry a fresh partner; perhaps one should say cohabit with him, as only the first marriage was sanctified by a priest.

As long as confidence was not upset, illegitimate children, too, were no impediment to a marriage. The scholar of Maya, Sylvanus G. Morley concluded: "It was not any more difficult for a young woman with one or more illegitimate children to find a husband than for her more virtuous sisters."[23]

On the other hand, an adulteress could be turned out by the husband in the Maya community; she also was punished by being forbidden to marry again, while the deceived husband could do so at once. The children were entrusted to one or the other of the parents, according to arrangement. With the Aztecs the sons remained with the father, the daughters with the mother—another indication that with the Mayas women's rights were not so restricted as in other high civilizations. A girl might before her marriage have already had experience of several relationships like this, she might even have been a prostitute, without anyone taking exception. Vows professing her virginity were made voluntarily by the girl and contained no religious obligation.

South of the Mayan Country

In this context the countries lying further to the south have also to be considered.

In Nicaragua, where there was a striking dissimilarity between the two most powerful tribes, the Chorotegs and the Nicaraos, the attitude towards virginity was the same as with the Mayas. In the case of rape the culprit became the lifelong slave of the victim's parents. Escape from this legal punishment was impossible; attempted escape could be expiated by death alone.

Among the Chorotegs, the chief undertook the deflowering of the young girls. The chronicler Oviedo explains this custom, of which he had received an account from one of the princes when he upbraided him for "sleeping the greatest part of his nights with a chaste girl, a great sin and a dreadful thing in the eyes of God; and further, for having many wives instead of one, which alone would be decent, and this even without counting those whom he deflowers." As in other parts of America, polygamy was habitual among the ruling families of the gold countries; this is indicated by the reply of the prince, who told the Spaniard "that he would be much happier with one wife than with so many; but the parents brought him their daughters and implored him to take them; he was doing it only so as to have many sons. And as far as the girls were concerned, he was doing it so as to honour them, for afterwards they would be sought as wives by the Indians far more eagerly than before."[24]

Owing to his social position, the *kazike* was able to afford several wives. The more sons he had, the greater was his influence. He could use them to fill the most important political, clerical and military posts.

At the marriage of the daughter the father gave the bridegroom a piece of his land. The dowry of the young girl, already fairly large, was further increased by her asking her suitors, when she wanted to be married, to build a house for her. At first, however, she kept the name of the chosen suitor a secret. "And the young men start the work and build the house and see to it that not the least little thing is missing. Rather they even increase their attentions to the young girl . . . they deem it a great honour not to be dismissed by her, but to have the chance of being chosen from among so many competitors."[25]

When the house was ready and all admirers, friends and relatives had been invited to the wedding feast, the girl would apologize that she could not divide herself among them, and therefore had to ask them to understand that one only could be her marriage choice. Until that moment every one of them seems still to have entertained some hope; for, it is said to have happened, quite frequently, that a disdained suitor chose suicide as a way out of this unpleasant situation. Relatives and the friends of the victor celebrated until morning.

From this moment the wife remained faithful to the husband, "drew near to no other man, and ran the house as well as she could." The premarital sexual freedom of the women was followed during marriage by some further liberties which the chronicler indignantly describes: "I have never heard of a custom more appropriate to an amorous, sinful and depraved people than the following one, common with these Indians; at a certain, very important annual festival when many people assemble, it is the custom for the women to be completely free through the festivities, which last all night. They can copulate with whomsoever they want, and without any regard to social standing . . . When that night is over, nothing resembling it occurs again . . . but neither is there any punishment or jealousy."[26]

Contemporary observers were struck by the fact that the men of the Chorotegs were subservient to the women, did all kinds of work for them and were even sometimes beaten by them. In quarrels the man usually was the loser and was chased from the house, as it had been built by the woman's admirers.

The warlike Nicaraos, who gave their name to the present Republic of Nicaragua, held a quite different opinion with regard to virginity. They attached great importance to it; it had to be specially confirmed before marriage. If the bride were found to be no longer a

30

virgin, the bridegroom could return her to her father, who had chosen him for her.

As elsewhere in America, among the lower ranks in Panama close blood relationships were thought to be the only impediment to a marriage. In these thinly populated countries childlessness was taken as a reason for the exchange or the sale of a wife. On the other hand, abortions, which were punished with death by the Aztecs, were here quite common but could probably be undertaken only with the consent of the husband. Oviedo reports the opinions of newly married brides: "It is the old people who ought to bring children into the world; they themselves do not want to be so busily occupied as to forego their pleasures, besides children would make their breasts flabby, their breasts of which they are extremely proud, and which in fact are beautiful." It is impossible to find out today whether these were exceptional views, thought to be of interest by the chronicler, or whether they represented a frequently observed attitude.

In his *Historia general y natural de las Indias*, Oviedo also mentions the amorous behaviour of the noble ladies in Panama who so generously offered their favours, "they themselves say that noble persons must not refuse anything for which they are asked; only ill-mannered people do this."

In Venezuela, it was, according to Gómara, the duty of the priest to undertake the defloration. "When a young girl is to be married, the *piache* or priest must first sleep with her to safeguard the happiness of the young couple. The following day she is handed over to her husband."

In *Historia general de las Indias* Oviedo continues: "The venerable fathers undertake this, so as not to lose their preeminent position and the respect due to them, and the husband then feels more secure ..." The Spaniard added that the concubines of the kings were not subjected to this treatment. In this country it was the custom—as for example also with the Eskimos—to offer the guest the most beautiful of the wives of the host. "And when he leaves again and she wants to follow him, she herself can decide upon this without her husband interfering. If she stays, she is not treated badly; on the contrary, her husband has to love her all the more because she has done her duty with regard to his friend and yet she has not deserted himself."

The few Europeans who wrote about Colombia mention that all the inhabitants were married and that monogamy was the rule among the simple people. Marriage was based on the purchase of the woman. Shortly before the birth of a child the mother went on a pilgrimage to a place where the hero of this civilization had left a footprint on a rock. They scraped off some of the stone, mixed it with water and drank it.

Upon the birth of a child, an oracle was consulted, a process in which a ball of cotton, sprinkled with mother's milk, played a part.

As regards succession: with the Cuevas the son was the heir; with the Cauca tribes the son of the sister inherited. With the Chibcha, the son of the chief's sister, too, was the heir to the throne. In contrast to this matriarchal succession among the ruling families, among common people the sons were also able to inherit.

WOMEN OF THE INCAN EMPIRE

The tribes of the Quechuas and of the Aymaras became the support of the empire of the Incas. There were in old Peru a number of other peoples, who developed distinct civilizations. In the last hundred and fifty years before the Spanish conquest, the dynasty of the Incas, belonging to the tribe of the Quechuas, succeeded in forming a political unity and a general standardization, as did the Aztecs in Mexico.

The Individual and the State

The Indian lived and died where he was born. The state was so thoroughly organized that the subject lacked any individuality; the rank was more important than the individual, who was absorbed in his tribe. Fond of his soil, the Indian usually lived from birth to death in the *ayllu* in which he had first seen the light. The *ayllu*, originally a group formed by family connections like the early clans, became in Peru the central unit of the community. Under certain circumstances, a woman was able to change through marriage to her husband's *ayllu*, but this did not happen often. The obligation to the *ayllu*, the nucleus of the state, was as strict as that to the family. In the empire of the Incas, man resembled one minute wheel among millions, a wheel which, however, was necessary to keep the whole machine working. Officials were appointed to control the geared system of wheels, to register everybody according to social standing, age and sex, to record how many couples were to be married, to keep track of each cultivated field and its harvest and how it was disposed of. All this—and more—was systematically recorded in the *quipu*, by the *quipuca-mayoc*, or "keeper of the knotted strings." Groups of individuals, goods, and so on were represented by strings of different colours; quantities were indicated by knots tied at specified intervals in the *quipu*. They were recorded in decimal fashion, the lowest knots on a string representing units, the next tens, then hundreds and thousands.

Thus new-born children, people ready to be married, those liable to military service and those of advanced age were registered by the state officials with small knots "as if with paper and ink." Without this statistical expedient it would have been impossible to make a survey of the empire which was comparable in size with that part of Europe that extends from Spitzbergen to Tunis. Poma de Ayala goes so far as to say that the empire was ruled by the *quipu*. Another chronicle affirms that not even a pair of sandals could be lost in this mighty empire without the officials of the Inca being informed of it.

Apart from its unique talent for organization, the society of the Incas was distinguished by its care for the future. Every newcomer *(mosoc caparic)* was registered. With the birth of each child, the state allotted the family more of the common land *(ayllu)*, a larger piece for a boy than for a girl. Some of the chroniclers mention a double grant. This reflects the fact that men, between the ages of 25 and 50, formed the most important citizen category, the most valuable group for the state.

In the empire of the Incas woman was a labourer and a guarantee of propagation. Like man, she was free and unfree. She had the same duties with regard to the state and was in return guaranteed the same protection. As the woman shared her fate with everybody of her rank, it was well-nigh impossible for her to leave the social order.

Pregnancy and Childbirth

As soon as the Indian woman knew herself to be pregnant, she prayed to the konopa and increased her offerings. The konopa were small domestic gods to whom the simple Indian felt closer than to the great gods worshipped in the temples. Their images were formerly to be found in every hut and can even today be seen here and there, wrapped up side by side with a faded print of a Catholic saint or the Virgin. Frequently images of the konopa were given as offerings to the dead together with the latter's tools or with food.

The Indian woman's work, even her heavy manual work, was in no way changed during her pregnancy. The Peruvian woman's delivery might well take place in the field or on the way home. She severed the umbilical cord with her finger-nails or with her teeth. Then the new-born was washed by its mother in the nearest river or watercourse, even at a height of 4000 metres. The Indians thought that this would harden the child. The mother treated the child tenderly only in so far as she did not at once plunge it into the ice-cold water, but took the water first into her mouth to warm it and then sprinkled the child with it. At home, the infant was tied to a kind of board cradle which could be used lying as well as standing, so that the mother could always take the child and its bed with her. The board had two narrow

sideboards and stood on four short blocks, those at the head-end somewhat longer, so that the child was not lying stretched out quite flat.

A premature birth was looked upon as a great calamity. To avoid it, magicians were called who, in a long ceremony, prayed to the gods to protect the embryo. The magician rubbed two or three stones of the size of a human palm against a piece of silver. Then he laid powdered cocoa leaves, cinnabar, or grated seashells on the stones. Next to the silver he put guinea-pigs and vessels filled with chicha.[27]

There were rules for the making of this ceremonial chicha; the maize had to be chewed by maidens or by women who had remained chaste while doing so, and who had not partaken of any salt or pepper during that time.

Then the magician rubbed the belly of the pregnant woman with the konopa. When he had done this, he put the idol on a bed of straw and prayed to it. In the further course of the ceremony he interrogated the sun; he threw objects into the air and saw from the position in which they fell whether or not his question had been answered in the affirmative. Several huacas[28] too were invoked. If the gods answered in the affirmative he knew which demons pursued the yet unborn child. Now it was important to propitiate them; cinnabar and the dust of the shells were entrusted to the winds, a guinea-pig was killed, and its lungs examined to see whether the sacrifice had turned out satisfactorily. In any case the magician started with a negative expectation. It happened frequently that more animals had to be slaughtered to gain certainty. At the end of the ceremony chicha was poured out to propitiate all evil spirits. Weak infants were given a piece of their own umbilical cord as a teat.

Child-rearing and Education

After the birth, the father was ordered to fast strictly. During the first days, he had to stay with his wife, not to help her but to frighten away evil spirits.

Children formed the sole wealth of these Indians, and it is therefore surprising that after their birth, their parents took them quite for granted, took little care of them while they grew up, and paid no attention to any hygienic precautions.

At first the parents gave the child a temporary name, for instance, "Fat Tommy," "Light Wind" or "Red

Earth"—a name with reference either to the first impression the child made or to the place where it had been born.

In the empire of the Incas it was strictly forbidden to the parents to take their child in their arms during the first months and to fondle it. It could be spoiled by this. If the mother returned on the third day to her usual activity, she took with her the infant together with its cradle. To give it the breast—most children were partly breast-fed until their third year—she bent over it, avoiding any fondling embrace, which was not allowed. Further, it was forbidden to suckle the child more than three times a day. Even among the privileged classes the whole care of the child was the duty of the mother alone.

All these severe and detailed rules were based not so much on tradition but on decrees of the Incas. Only when the child had to learn to crawl and later to run, was it freed from the fetters of its cradle and laid on a rug which lay in a hollow of the earth in the hut. Even then the mother was not allowed to take it in her arms when she wanted to suckle it; she had to bend over the child, who was to be lying down.

According to the classification in the chronicle of Poma de Ayala, which is not quite identical with the traditions of earlier reporters, the "cradle-child" was followed by the "child able to stand alone" (saya huamarac). During this "time of play," between the first and the fifth year, it had, as Cabeza de Vaca reported, to "pick lice out of the hair so as not to be unoccupied."[29] From the fifth to the ninth year it was the "child able to walk" (macta puric). Between the ninth and the twelfth year the range of its duties was increased: being a "bread receiver" it had to chase the birds out of the maize fields.

Neither the young girls nor the boys had any idea how limited were the chances awaiting them in this great and well organized state. While the boy had no choice but to learn the trade of his father, there was for the girl one slim possibility of breaking out of her rank; that was when the official, who recruited the young men for the army and the public works, took notice of her. One of his duties was to choose the most beautiful girls of the country for service in the temple and for the personal requirements of the imperial family. But the chances of her being selected were not more than one in a thousand.

Though there were in the capital many schools and numerous teachers, or amautus, only the children of nobles were entrusted to them. The following typical Inca maxim is attributed to Túpac Yupanqui, the tenth Inca: "Knowledge is not for the people, but for those of noble blood." The Inca Garcilaso de la Vega reported of Roca, the sixth Inca, that, after his conquests, he issued many laws for the public safety, forbade excesses of any kind and founded in Cuzco, the "Navel of the world" (as the capital of the Inca empire was called), an academy for the education of the imperial princes. "One ought to teach the sciences to nobles only, not to the children of lowly people, since one would risk making them proud by giving them such lofty knowledge, and that might harm the state. To occupy these people it would suffice if each learned his father's (or his mother's) trade." These laws were not known to the simple Indians, nor were they aware of their consequences.

Ceremony of Naming

The first major event in a girl's life was the ceremony of giving her a name. The ceremony took place between her fifth and her twelfth year; the family assembled and chose the godfather. He began the ceremony with a knife of flint with which he cut the hair and the nails of the child. Drinking copious quantities of chicha as at all similar festivities, the godfather gave the flint knife to the members of the family, all of whom took part in the cutting. The mother carefully kept the hair and the nails, as there was a widespread superstition that their possession might bestow on its holder the power to influence the child's life. In some districts, hair and nails were taken into the huaca (sacred building) of the ayllu.

The child's name was usually composed of the name of the huaca and that of a special event. The chronicler Ariaga reported: "There is, however, no small child who does not know the name of the huaca of its tribe." Thus, in the name of Paucar Libiac, "Paucar" refers to the sanctuary of the ayllu and "Libiac" commemorates a flash of lightning which struck near a child, still quite small, who escaped unhurt.

After this brief festivity, which ended with dancing, singing and a drinking bout, everyday life started again. But the young girl, though still a child, from now on was a full member of the community of the ayllu, and, in case of her early death, was entitled to be buried in the tomb of her ancestors. She had now to help her mother

34

SEGVNDA CALLE
PAIA·CONA

de dat de un cuenta años

muger q̃ sirue al principal   cnos ta

in the house, and was already being taught the woman's most important skill, spinning and weaving. The best weavers were found in pre-Spanish Peru. Every kind of weaving known to us today was already practised in the pre-Inca civilization; experts have counted more than one hundred and ninety different colours and shades of colour. The favourable climate, especially that of the southern coast which is almost devoid of rainfall, combined with the practice of burying objects with the dead, helped to preserve these materials; together with those of the Copts in Egypt, they are the most ancient and beautiful that have come down to us from the great civilizations of the past(Ill. 109, 112).

Young people between the ages of eight and fifteen were entered by the officials in the "knot records" as *puclac huarma*, that is as "the youth still inclined to play." The boys had to hire themselves out as llama shepherds or as apprentices; the girls helped their mothers at the hearth, in the fields and at the loom. To this period belongs the second and last great event previous to marriage.

Coming of Age

The start of menstruation was the occasion for a celebration. The parents recalled once again to the young girl all her duties to them and to her superiors. As initial preparation for this festivity of puberty the girl had to fast for forty-eight hours. On the third day, her food consisted of a few uncooked maize kernels. On the fourth day, she could take off the garments of childhood, and she received from her mother those of a woman; her hair was no more to fall loosely over her forehead, but was plaited; and then she was given her woman's name.

Different, however, was the destiny of those girls whom the official envoy of the Inca had previously selected to enter religious service and to spend their lives in one of the "houses of the chosen." The chosen girls were separated for life from their parents; neither the father nor the mother had the right to object. One of the chroniclers reports that these young girls "had to be virgins, and so as to make quite sure of this, they were chosen before they were eight years old." Their position was somewhat similar to that of the vestals in ancient Rome. Besides the worship of the sun, they had practical duties; they made the priceless garments worn by the imperial family. The majority of the "chosen" were daughters of high officials and were of noble descent.

Marriage

The young girls in ancient Peru usually were married at eighteen to twenty-two years of age; the young men were usually entitled to take a wife only when twenty-five. (In Mexico young girls were rarely more than eighteen when they married, the men about twenty.) With the marriage the Indian girl left the protection and care of her parents. In the empire of the Incas, the wedding festivities were not so full of ceremony as those in ancient Mexico. The wedding was simply an administrative event without any religious ceremony. This can partly be explained by the fact that in the states on the Pacific coast virginity was not greatly valued. Pater Cobo states in his *Historia del Nuevo Mundo* (Book XI): "Virginity is looked upon as a blemish, since the Indians maintain that only those remain virgins who cannot manage to be loved by anybody." It even was the bitterest reproach to which the wife had to listen in a matrimonial quarrel if the husband could say: "You had not even had a lover before we married." It was quite different with the Aztecs, who usually preferred chaste women for wives.

At the time of the Incas, marriage on probation for two or three years was not rare. If the wife then returned to her parents, either because the husband did not please her or because he was a drunkard, or if he sent her back because she did not fulfil his expectations as a lover or, still more important, as a housewife or a labourer, this did not involve any loss in her moral reputation. For a young girl it was in any case honourable to be sought for a trial marriage.

Marriage was a practical affair for the lower classes in the empire of the Incas. Once a year an inspector came to the *ayllu* as the representative of the Inca. He made the young men stand up in a line; facing them, also in a line, stood the young girls. The official asked whether they were willing to be married and whether there had already been any trial marriage. He took care that the couples to be married were not blood relations but that they were of the same social rank.

Usually, the marriage had already been decided upon by the parents, and the young couples tried to arrange to stand facing each other. Young men who yet had no bride were asked by the official to choose one of the maidens. If they hesitated, he allotted one to them. Marriage was a duty, as the economic wealth of the state and part of its military power depended upon the size

of the population. This marriage was recognized as the final one. Divorce or separation were possible only if the wife remained childless.

The dowry was small; wool, a spindle, a spindle whorl, a poncho needle, tools for weaving, perhaps a shell as a pendant or a chain of painted clay beads for festivities.

Among the Aztecs, an adulteress was punished with death by stoning, and the husband merely threatened with the same punishment *de iure*. In ancient Peru, however, both partners qualified for the death sentence. The orally transmitted laws state: "Adultery damages the reputation and the standing of one's neighbor, creates uncertainty and alarm. The adulterer is a thief and is therefore to be put to death without much ado." The death sentence was provided also for rape. But if, notwithstanding the violation, the girl was still able to find a husband, the punishment was remitted, since the general welfare was not endangered; celibacy was not to be tolerated as it would have become a burden to the state.

All this could easily create the impression that the Peruvians were unfeeling people, were it not that other literary sources prove the contrary. Even their languages, especially Aymara and Quechua, give the lie to this superficial impression by their great number of endearing pet names, which can have been invented only by a lover for his beloved; for instance, Cusi Coyllur (Star of Joy).

The few love songs too, which have been in part preserved for us by the Inca Garcilaso de la Vega, testify to the deep feelings of these highly reserved Quechua Indians.

"Flowers,
  Surrounding the maize fields,
Flowers,
  Opening their calices
As you open your lips.
I want to be
Like the humming bird,
Who assails the flowers.
How loving you were
Little dove.
Then,
When I found myself in the reflection
Of your eyes,
Radiant eyes,
In the uncanny night,
Sending over me flashes of lightning."

In an ancient fable,[30] to be retold here in a few words, the folk found their own language, showed their secret thoughts, hopes and fears.

"High up in the mountains there lived two people with their child. The husband frequently went away travelling and left his wife alone with the child. She often was awake all through the night, sewing and weaving; continually tears trickled down over her face, which the child, however, noticed only occasionally. Once when he could not fall asleep, he asked his mother what it was that fluttered about there, and to which she was speaking. 'It is my lover, my affectionate friend, who keeps me company,' was the mother's reply.

"When the man came back home and the wife had gone to the field, he began to talk to the child. He asked what the mother had been doing while he was away and the child told him that the mother's lover came every night and that she stayed up late so as to talk to him.

"Hearing this, the husband looked for his wife and killed her. One night, given up to his sad memories, he could not sleep and lay there staring into the dim light shining from the fire in the hearth. Suddenly the child called out: 'Here is mother's lover, who always visited her and to whom she spoke at night,' and saying this he pointed to a large moth: 'That is the one who always came when mother could not sleep.'

"The man realized his mistake, gave himself up to despair and died of a broken heart."

One of the chroniclers writes about the woman of Peru: "She was an object and was treated as such." This kind of misjudgment by the Spanish chroniclers was not uncommon, and was probably due to the fact that the Indians showed their feelings very little. The significance of the reserved Indian's small gestures and modest traditions would be lost on the inattentive observer. The ceremonial aspect of a marriage was meagre—it was accomplished, for the Inca official, merely by the pressure of the hand; but this was accompanied by a small loving gesture: the new husband pushed his sandals towards his wife.

Owing to the practice of trial marriages, it is safe to assume that "love matches" were not unusual. The old people, in attempting to hand down their wisdom to the young couples, would advise them: "You now are married, you must work together, as you have cooked together" (a previous marriage on approval was here being taken for granted); "you will both be in love, as it is not good if one cools off while the other is still consumed by burning passion."

After the marriage, the wife moved into her husband's house. The *ayllu* (the local community) gave to the young couple a piece of the communal land. Since the land belonged to the community, one third of the yield fell to the Inca (i.e., the state) who had to care for his subjects in case of famine; another third belonged to the sun, that is, the priests, because the sun was worshipped as the supreme deity, and the priests had to build new temples and to maintain the cult. Only the last third of the yield was at the disposal of the Indian for himself and his family.

The right of succession usually applied to only a very small inheritance, as the right of private property was restricted. In the tribe of the Chibcha, on the central coast, the father could in his will designate as heirs not only his sons but other relatives as well. The will was made orally in the presence of witnesses. An ancient matriarchy existed where the brother or son of a sister inherited, or where the succession of the wife seemed to be reasonable. Usually, however, the wife was left empty-handed.

Money as a means of payment in our sense was unknown in pre-Spanish Peru. Work represented value for the state, work being an obligation, a duty of the individual, which, on the other hand, implied the duty of the state to protect its subjects from their enemies and to care sufficiently for them in case of famine, infirmity or old age. The communal holding of land, the restrictions on private property, the obligation to work and the care taken by the state of each individual have of course led to comparisons of the Incas' system with modern socialism.[31]

CLOTHING, COSMETICS AND HAIR STYLES

When the first Europeans came to the countries in which high civilizations had been established, they found there no "naked savages," but met people who did not think less highly of garments, jewelry and cosmetics than any inhabitant of old Europe. If we look through the ancient picture-writings of the Aztecs and Mixtecs, and then observe the Indian women on the market-day in the remote villages of Mexico, we notice that very little has changed with regard to their basic garments. Comparing those with the offerings in the graves, one even finds colours and ornaments similar to those of the pre-Spanish period. The men replaced the loin-cloth *(maxtlatl)* with trousers, but in the clothing of the women of the Aztecs, and in Peru, even the most prudish missionaries could not discover anything improper. Their reports mention, and even praise, the richly embroidered shirts and skirts of the women.

The clothing of the women consisted mainly of three pieces. This is the case even today in the more distant villages of the regions where the advanced civilizations of the Aztecs, Mayas and Incas flourished. The shirt, called *huipilli* in Aztec, was made of two straight widths of material. There were slits at the seams to leave openings for the arms. To let the head pass through, there was a slit the edges of which were usually decorated with some trimming. To this was added a skirt (in Aztec, *cueitl*; in the language of the Mayas, *pic*), a cloth of about two metres in length; this was wrapped round the hips. In front it was folded to provide freedom of movement, while at the back it was tautly stretched over the buttocks. It was held by a long closely woven ribbon, usually of approximately a hand's breadth, which was decorated with multi-coloured motifs. On their feet, men and women wore sandals; often great pains were taken to ornament them richly and in good taste.

The Mexican woman rarely wore any headdress, but she was skilled at setting off her deep black hair with coloured ribbons and cords which she plaited into her tresses. She also liked to wear a finely woven coloured fillet. Only in the high mountains of the central Andes a hat was added to the cap, differing from the broad brimmed hats worn nowadays by Indian women of Peru and Bolivia. As can be seen from the ceramics, the female headdress often consisted of a scarf wound round the head, whereas the headdress of the men was more handsome and richly decorated.

In the highlands of the vast continent, with their

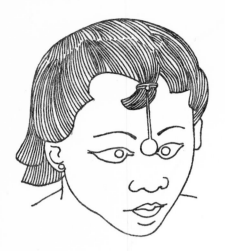

Correcting the position of the eyes. The so-called "silver look"
was an ideal of beauty among the Maya Indians
(after Alberto Beltran)

sparse vegetation, the colour contrasts of the soil consist only of different shades of brown; man seemed therefore particularly anxious to make up for this monotony with colourful garments. The chief jewelry for men and women was necklaces and other chains, and a kind of earplug made of a great variety of materials such as painted clay and delicately worked jade (Ill. 57, 58).

In the Maya region the clothing of the women usually consisted also of a long skirt of wool or cotton *(pic)*, usually wrapped round the hips and held below the breasts by a broad belt. The richly decorated blouse *(kub)* was worn in this very hot climate only on festive days or for solemn occasions; otherwise the upper part of the body was covered with only a plain cotton shirt, or was bare. For ceremonial occasions the Maya woman wore a wrap that resembled a toga. It was made in a variety of patterns and could be varied still further by the way it was draped. Frequently the front part was shorter than that covering the back. Patterns and colours varied from district to district, as they do even today. It was therefore easy to tell where the wearer came from. Some young girls wore the wrap slightly open in front, while others preferred slits at the sides. A particularly richly embroidered skirt, decorated with various ornaments, was provided for ceremonial occasions. The making of garments was exclusively the work of women.

The social rank of any woman was obvious to the world at large from the particular quality of her garments and especially from her jewelry—her necklaces, bracelets and anklets, earplugs and nose-rings—and more so still from the care vouchsafed to her hairdressing; moreover, the Maya noble women wore artistic headdresses, looking somewhat like turbans or broad-brimmed hats.

The terracottas from Jaina, the famous pottery centre of the New World (Ill. 82–91), can give us an idea of the elegance of the Mayas. Most of this pottery is from the graves of Jaina, the island of the dead in the Gulf of Campeche. Owing to their power of expression and their importance as archeological finds, these works of art are among the most notable that have come down to us from the late classical period of this high civilization. An element in the standard of beauty was the "ideal profile," forehead and nose forming an unbroken line. The heads of infants were pressed between two boards to make the forehead flat, by frontal occipital deformation. The Peruvians bound the infants' heads tightly, thus forming the elongated head, which fitted their taste. The Maya mother hung a bead before the child's eyes to teach it to squint; the so-called "silver look," the squint, a flat forehead and a long, slightly curved nose constituted the most prized type of beauty.

To achieve a still greater harmony between nose and forehead, that is, to make it look as if the nose rose out of the forehead, a piece of rubber was inserted under the skin between the nose and forehead in order to extend the bridge of the nose. The Mayas were round-headed and had large almond-shaped eyes; their long narrow noses were emphasized by these cosmetic operations.

The ideal of beauty with regard to garments and jewelry, which made no distinction between the sexes, makes it often impossible to identify the richly clad dignitaries on the steles. As with the Aztecs, modesty prevented the representation of nakedness. In ceramics and vase painting, physical distinctions of sex were seldom explicitly indicated.

In the empire of the Incas the women's clothing con-

40

sisted of a long tunic *(anacu)* of llama wool, held together by a multi-coloured belt; the tunic was slit on one side to make walking easier. A grey shawl *(lliclla)*, also of llama wool, was worn over it; it was fastened in front by a pin with a large head. This pin, made of silver, pewter or bronze, was one of the few pieces of jewelry of the common Peruvian woman.

The state controlled all clothing, and regulations were strictly observed. On his wedding-day, the Indian received two garments, one for everyday use, the other for festive days. They were worn until they fell completely to pieces. According to the evidence of thousands of excavations the most beautiful garments, excepting those of the rulers, were reserved for the dead.

Women usually still wore plain sandals *(usuta)* of llama leather. For everyday use, there were also bands or straps worn on head or chest as supports for burdens. There were, further, small pouches with geometrical ornaments or stylized bird or llama motifs; they were worn over the shoulder or round the neck (Ill. 105). As the simple and uniform clothing could not be altered without official permission, the young girls and women had recourse to decorating their hair with coloured ribbons and trying to attract attention to their slim necks with small necklaces of coloured stones or pieces of seashells.

In the coastal districts and in the eastern primeval forests of Peru, clothing was used solely as a protective measure and covered only the few most sensitive parts of the body. Its pattern also served, however, to make clearly apparent the social rank of the wearer. On the northern coast it was mainly the headdress that indicated differences of social rank; it varied from a simple cloth to a conical cap (Ill. 45). Here, as in all tropical regions, nakedness had no moral implication; it was neither dishonourable nor did it offend decency.

Identification of sex in Inca art is made particularly difficult by the fact that women and men of the higher ranks wore the same jewelry: a chain of jade beads, shells or jaguar-bones and earplugs. Those who could afford it had the last-named made of thinly cut and highly polished green jade. Jade and jadeite were more precious than gold. The technique of winning and working gold became known in the country of the Mayas not earlier than the tenth to twelfth centuries.

In the gold countries proper, Nicaragua, Costa Rica, and Panama—and in some of the tropical parts of

Venezuela and Colombia, nakedness was the rule. Columbus who sailed on his fourth journey (1502–1504) along the coast from the Isthmus of Panama to the Gulf of Honduras, trying to find a passage, noted: "These people, men and women, are as naked as when their mothers brought them into the world. The women wear something made of cotton to hide their sex, but nothing else." The "thing made of cotton" was an apron, approximately twenty centimetres wide, worn loose or tied tightly with a cord around the waist, and as Oviedo says in his *Historia general*, "loose in front of their private parts, it was at the mercy of the wind." In those tropical zones in which no higher civilization developed, the breasts remained uncovered. From Colombia the same chronicler reports "a kind of loose breeches, which in even the very slightest wind hide nothing." This article of clothing corresponded to the kind of loin cloth *(maxtlatl)* worn in Mexico by men, but this used to be securely girded.

Of the north of Venezuela Oviedo reported: "The women wear trousers, made of a two-span wide piece of material, held by a cord which they use to gird themselves. This piece of material covers their hips, and is passed through between the legs and fastened to the same belt, so that it covers the privy parts and the belly. All the rest of the body is left bare." The married women showed their state by a multi-coloured cord worn crossed over the breasts. After their first intercourse, they also altered their garments, now usually wearing a small apron or short skirt which reached about a hand's breadth above the knee. Noble ladies preferred a skirt covering the calves, and sometimes, according to the wearer's rank, this garment reached down to the ankles. In Colombia, in the *tierra fría*, higher up in the mountains, the breasts were covered with a richly decorated shawl, while in Panama the Spaniards were surprised to see the ladies wearing a kind of breastplate made of delicately wrought sheets of gold and frequently decorated with religious motifs. In these sheets weighing up to two hundred ounces, there were holes through which a string was passed, so that they could be worn hanging from the shoulders. Oviedo says that "these gold-plates, invented to lift the breasts, enhance the refinement of feminine clothing worn by the noble ladies of the Gulf of Urabá." In the Cauca Valley of Colombia, disc-like imitations of female breasts were found, which probably had been sewn on shirts or blouses.

The well-cared-for hair of the young girls and women was worn uncovered in these regions. Exceptions were the women of Cartagena (Colombia) who adorned themselves with gold diadems, and those of some districts in Central Colombia, who enhanced their beauty by wearing a multi-coloured wreath, with a flower on the forehead. In Nicaragua, combs of stag-bones supported the coiffures of the women.

From the earliest times, restraint had hardly anywhere been shown in the use of make-up for the face or for the body. Varying from tribe to tribe, make-up usually served to indicate social standing. Excavations show that ornaments were frequently used to draw attention to the small breasts of coquettish young women (Ill. 94). Only seldom do chroniclers mention the painting of the body. In Colombia, the face was painted with oil or petroleum in a variety of colours, and the body in vermillion. In this connection Oviedo states specifically: "The women paint themselves in the same manner; the higher their rank, the more they are painted." In Nicaragua, it was the custom to paint the arms, oddly enough, with a black paint made of a mixture of coal and of one's own blood; this symbolized the fur of the jaguar. Diego de Landa mentions a habit of painting the upper part of the body with petroleum, but omitting the breasts of the women, possibly so as not to interfere with the suckling of children.

The teeth of the Indians are beautiful by nature, but in Peru the women of higher rank used a special technique to make the gums look redder and the teeth thereby more brilliant. Boiling hot herbs were put on the mucous membranes to inflame them. For days the woman could take only liquid food; then the scalded skin detached itself and the gums shone bright red.

FOOD AND COOKING

The realm of the woman was the kitchen. When she was not helping her husband in the fields, she had to take her place at the hearth or behind the millstone *(metate)*. The traveller who today enters an Indian hut situated off the beaten track, will, without fail, at first gain the impression that here nothing has been changed—apart from a few cheap tins and a calendar with a faded print. The hut is still as simple as it was two thousand years ago, consisting of one windowless room. Here time has passed without leaving a trace; the woman stands at the millstone, the fire smoulders between the three hearthstones, the fan of plaited palm leaves fans the glow and, not least, children dressed only in little shirts romp about on the clay floor.

The same applies to the food as to the hut. We owe the existence of more than half of our foodstuffs to the New World. Probably, in Mexico and Peru a greater variety of edible plants, spices and medicinal herbs has been cultivated than in any other country: the maize which with its twenty varieties provides the second largest quantity of food to the world; the potato, with approximately two hundred and forty varieties; the sweet potato *(butate);* innumerable kinds of marrows and beans; yam, manioc (cassava, a tuber plant), chili (capsicum), tomatoes, cucumbers, peanuts, cashew nuts, pineapples, cocoa, red pepper, papaw. These have been naturalized in the Old World since the era of the conquests and their Indian origin is often forgotten. The only important foodstuffs of the world unknown to the Indians were rice, wheat, barley and millet. That the Indians have even today not become used to these "foreign" foodstuffs, shows how conservative their cooking is. The Indian does not take to anything that has not been produced by his soil ever since early times; coffee and cane sugar are the sole exceptions.

In Mexico and in the lands of the Mayas maize was at all times the main food. Diego de Landa, the second bishop of Yucatán, wrote: "Truly, they almost make a god of it," and he was not wrong. The welfare of the people depended upon its growth and health. No wonder, therefore, that the maize gods occupied a large space in the pantheon of the Mayas and the Aztecs.

The maize-eaters of Mesoamerica did not have to cope with any problem of preservation. There were varied ways to stretch one year's harvest to the next. Maize is still today for the Indian peasant the same as wheat for the European. Maize is bread; this bread of the Mexicans has always been and is still today formed into flat cakes (called in Aztec *tlaxcalli*), today mistakenly called *tortilla* (the Spanish name for pancake), though they are made only of boiled maize, water and a little salt. In Peru, the potato was likewise very important. It grew and thrived in the hot zone of the coast as well as on the perpetually clouded mountain slopes of the Cordilleras; but unlike other foodstuffs, it was rather perishable. The Peruvians, therefore, invented means of food preservation. They exposed the potatoes to the cold of the night, and stamped on them the next morning till they had squeezed out all liquid. The product of this process, which was turned into a kind of flour, was called *chuño*. It was one of the most important foodstuffs stored in the Incas' granaries as a reserve for emergencies.

Besides the maize, the small black beans were important; they could be prepared as food in various ways. To this food, consisting mainly of carbohydrates, were added chili pods (capsicum), a small near relation of the paprika-family. It was almost the only food containing vitamin C. Meat and fish dishes depended on the individual region, and did not play an important role in the Indian kitchen; they were usually a matter of chance, that is, hunter's luck. The Indians, who were, with few exceptions, vegetarians, reserved meat dishes for festive occasions. The scarcity of meat was due in part to the fact that the men who achieved so much in cultivating useful plants, were less successful as breeders of food animals because of the lack of species suitable for domestication.

There was little meat and not much variety in what was available for the woman to prepare. Usually only the turkey, bred on the farm itself, was available to her unless, of course, her husband had previously exchanged it in the market for pulque. Sometimes, she could fall back upon fattened dogs or guinea-pigs, or upon her husband's luck as a hunter. In the central districts of the Andes the llama was a domestic animal; it, however, was only very rarely slaughtered since it was more useful as a beast of burden and provided the wool for clothing. Moreover, its dung could be used as fuel. The Aztec woman could send her children to the cactus fields to collect maguay worms, or to the rivers and lagoons to catch crabs and frogs. If she lived in Tenochtitlán or in one of the villages all round the Lake of Texcoco, her children looked for the larvae of the water lizard. All these rather exotic foodstuffs were valued delicacies, especially as the Indian woman was well versed in preparing unusual dishes. Thus,

chocolatl, the cocoa bean, was cooked not with sugar but with the savoury capsicum pepper. Apart from cocoa, she had at her disposal vanilla and various seeds for seasoning. She did not know sugar, but used wild honey.

As an intoxicating drink at festivities, pulque was very popular in Mexico, and chicha in the region of the Andes. The former was obtained from the juice of the pulque agave, a variety of the agava cactus; the latter was made from chewed maize kernels. Pulque, still today a popular drink with the Mexican Indian, looks like buttermilk and tastes like pale ale. It contains various nutritious constituents, and is very wholesome when consumed in small quantities. In ancient times the drinking of this beverage was regarded as making part of a religious ceremony. Four beakers only were allowed; the fifth was deemed to be excessive, and young people were severely punished for taking it.

Let us now also consider the narrow range of kitchen utensils with which the Indian woman had to make do, and with which for the most part she still manages today. The most important item in her hut—apart from the hearth—was the millstone, a volcanic stone, slightly vaulted (cylinder-shaped). It was called *metlatl* or *metlapilli*, the "son of the millstone," and served to grind the maize into a dry meal-like substance until no kernel was left visible.

The *metate*, as it is called today, was the main implement for making the Indians' bread. In addition to earthenware pots, the Indian woman used shallow crucibles of clay. There was also a bowl of stone, usually standing on three feet, with a fluted pattern scratched inside. This was the utensil with which the woman made the *chilmulli*, that is, the various sauces. There were additional mortars to pound roots, and some richly decorated cups and plates. Many an implement in the household of the Indian woman was of more perishable material, for example, baskets and sieves made from the fruit of the calabash tree, flasks from pumpkins and cups from various fruits. Palm leaves were used to make fans to kindle the fire, and there were wooden chocolate whisks. In most areas these items have not survived from pre-Spanish times, but we find some of them, of the same or very similar make, in today's Indian kitchen. In Peru, because of the climate, even very small delicate objects have survived for nearly two thousand years, for example little sewing boxes, sewing needles of cactus thorns, spinning implements and combs of wood (Ill. 101).

44

PROSTITUTION AND ORGIASTIC RELIGION

Prostitution

Various reports have been left by Spanish chroniclers. The Maya Indians mention prostitution but without giving any details. In Nicaragua, among the Chorotegs, it was the custom for young girls to earn their living and to increase their dowry with fees—ten cocoa beans—from casual lovers. The parents, in whose houses the girls lived until they were married, accepted this custom. The prostitutes used a special part of the market for their profession. They suffered no loss of prestige by selling their bodies; they were even respected because of doing so. Oviedo mentions that young men accompanied them like any other female workers or employees, on the way to and from their work. The chronicler refers to these young men as "pimps," and he mentions repeatedly that they received neither money nor any special favour from the girls. Prostitution ended with the wedding day.

Of Peru we learn only through a few lines by Garcilaso de la Vega: "The prostitutes, tolerated by the Incas only so as to avoid worse evils, lived outside the settlements in miserable huts, each of them alone and separated from the others. They were not allowed to enter the village, so as not to contact other women."

We know of similar moral concepts among the Aztecs. Here, our knowledge of the general attitude toward prostitution comes again from the tireless Franciscan Fra Sahagún. Owing to the metropolitan character of the capital of Tenochtitlán, its wealth on the one hand and the too rapidly growing population on the other, as well as to the poverty of the lower classes living on the outskirts, a society developed which stimulated ambitious desires, and which was basically different from that of the peasants. Money was unknown to this society, but there were sufficient equivalents with which to acquire and to increase riches.[32] Prostitution was not forbidden by law but, contrary to the attitude of the Chorotegs in Nicaragua, it was thoroughly condemned. It was not the man who made use of it, however, who was despised, but the woman who took it up as a job, since for the Mexicans the body did not hide the inner soul but laid it bare. Thus, modesty had a defensive character, like the impenetrable wall of politeness which the Mexicans built up through elaborate verbosity. Self-restraint was thought the chief virtue of women as well as of men. There was in the everyday relations of men and women much restraint, ceremonial reserve and modesty, based on a sense of shame with regard to one's own as well as to other people's nakedness. With the Aztecs, it was almost a physical reflex which can be clearly observed in the representations of gods and men.

No document could provide a better picture than the description of a prostitute given by one of Sahagún's Aztec informants shortly after the conquest of Mexico:
"She who sells
The lower part of her body
Yes,
Sells it,
Is a prostitute.
She suffers much,
She has taken to drink;
Pulque
Carries her over
To the other life.
Disgustingly dressed up,
Disgustingly made up,
A woman of lust
Bargaining
With her body.
Business therefore is
The finery,
The pomp.
To the market she carries
Earth-coloured flesh,
Earth-coloured flesh,
Her own most particular possession,
Earth-coloured
Her shame.
A slovenly,
A bad woman
That's what she is,
Who spreads out
Her fawning
Unmistakable
Gestures
At the shore of the lake.
Half still a child,
Half a marriageable woman,
She smells badly,
The badly smelling woman.
Soon young,
Soon thirty,
Soon sixty,
A bad old woman,
Small
Yet full of lust.
Restless she stays at the water;
That's where she stops
With her lust.
To and fro
She saunters along the street,
Shows herself at the market,
Stains the market.
There she saunters about,
Lolls and sprawls.
Quarrels with women
And makes herself ready for men.
Nowhere is her home,
Nowhere
Can she make her bed;
Nowhere
Starts for her
The new day,
And it is impossible
For her to find rest
By day as by night."[33]

It is strange that the image of the "infamous" woman is nearly always connected with the idea of restlessness. She comes and goes, looks for men and leaves them. Unlike the selfless mother and the waiting bride, safeguarded by tradition, she finds no rest. It is not the finery, not the pomp, it is her shamelessness and her restlessness which turn her soul to stone. The "infamous" woman is hard, heartless and self-willed.

It is strange that this image of the prostitute could have developed while such an important role was entrusted to her: to entertain, even to form in her own way the young and immature pupils in the *telpochcalli*. Here we find again the dualism which we have seen in the images of the gods. Coatlicue, the goddess of love, is at the same time the goddess of sin.

Sexual Aspects of Religion

In the system of religious worship, public prostitutes played an essential part, comparable to that of the Bacchante of classical antiquity. Thus, it is reported that for the feast of Tlaxochimaco, the temple and the images of the gods were decorated with wreaths of flowers and that in the course of the festivity warriors copulated with public prostitutes as a kind of conjuration of fertility.

Some French sociologists hold that with this ritual debauch the community safeguarded itself against the envy of the gods and of men, just as sacrifices and gifts appease the gods and the saints, festivities and games the people. Excessive use of power, and waste, confirmed the wealth of the community; luxury was a guarantee of welfare—to exhibit it had magic power. Waste was to be infectious and attract true affluence. The waste of life in war as in sacrifice created new life.

Therefore, religious worship was closely connected with the prosperity of the crops in the fields. The Mayas, like the Chorotegs, mortified themselves by drawing blood and sprinkling it over the corn cobs. The same idea underlay the orgiastic festivities where young girls were sacrificed for the common weal and so as to avert disaster. In Nicaragua, they are said to have jumped voluntarily into the crater of the volcano Masaya, and on the peninsula of Yucatán they sacrificed themselves in the holy cenotaph of Chichén Itzá which was dedicated to Chac, the god of rain.

An erotic serpent dance is still found to be popular in some remote villages of the Quiché Indians in the highlands of Guatemala; it is called "breaking the maize." The ripe corn cobs are bent downwards to protect the harvest against rain and birds. The ceremony is executed by a dozen or more men, in their usual attire, but carrying rattles in their hands and having their faces covered with masks. One is disguised as a woman. This relic only gives a vague impression of the former cult elements of the dance.

On the previous day, the participants set out to collect the snakes whose hiding places had been marked by a priest. The jaws of the poisonous snakes were tied together, and then they were all carried together in a basket to the house of the man disguised as a woman. The ceremony itself started with opening dances by the men, so as to throw themselves into ecstasy. Then one after the other of the men took hold of the man representing a woman and made the gestures symbolizing coition while the latter was held by two or more others of the men. With orgiastic screams, obscene gestures and exclamations, the other dancers illustrated the symbolized act. During the dance the dancers whipped themselves mercilessly, taking the snakes out of the basket and putting them under their shirts. The snakes crawled out of the sleeves or the legs of the trousers, were collected and at the end of the ceremony were again set free.

Everywhere in Mesoamerica the snake symbolized rain and fertility. The rattles of the dancers represented the attributes of the earth gods; the magic rite of sexual copulation was intended to propitiate the gods so that they might give a good crop of maize.

WIVES OF THE RULERS

In contrast to the Inca couple, revered as holy, we seldom meet among the Aztec rulers a woman of whom anything has been reported historically. The difference between the two dynasties of Cuzco (Peru) and Tenochtitlán (Mexico) is due not so much to the character of the dynasties as to the historical memory of the neighboring vanquished and tributary people. While the dynasty of the Incas arose from among small Quechua tribes, settled in the vicinity of Cuzco, Aztecs penetrated in a relatively late period into the high valley of Mexico, where they were surrounded by tribes with a long past, still alive in the memory of these long established people. To establish Aztec descent from the semi-lengendary Toltecs, official historians had dressed up the family tree of the Aztecs with numerous fictitious titles of nobility and names of localities, thereby increasing the uncertainty concerning the origin of the Mexican rulers. For instance, the first historical ruler, Acamapichtli (1375–1395), had at all costs to be descended from the Toltecs.[34] And only here, at the foundation of the Aztec dynasty, a woman played an essential, though not very clearly understandable part. This is the "Señora" of the exalted Colhuacan family, who appears on the one hand as his adopted mother, and on the other hand as his wife. Through her, the descent from the Toltecs was established, and thereby were legalized the rights and claims on a highly developed civilization, on which the "upstarts," as the Americanist Disselhoff[35] called the Aztecs, had insisted. This well-known episode from the early history of Tenochtitlán seems to justify the assumption that in pre-Aztec Mexico, nobility and power were transmitted at least partly through the female line.

In later Aztec history little attention is paid to the wives of the rulers, except that, when mentioned, they are sometimes given charming names accompanied by brief descriptions like "beautiful," "delicate" or "fond of power." As consort of the ruler, the Aztec woman clearly occupied only a secondary place. As goddess in the pantheon of the Aztecs, where she was the opposite number, sometimes also the playmate, of a god, she could not so easily be deposed. Each successor of Acamapichtli had a principal wife, whose sons were claimants to the throne, and several concubines. The latters' children were entitled to offices of high rank. Moctezuma II, the last reigning "emperor" before the Spanish conquest, had, according to Gómara, more than one hundred concubines; according to the chronicler Torquemada, there

The Inca and his "Coya" in a litter (from Nueva Corónica y buen Gobierno by Poma de Ayala)

were in the imperial "harem" even more than three thousand.

To learn anything about the wives of the Mexican rulers one has to turn over some thousand pages in the ancient reports from early colonial times. In the *Historia Chichimeca* of the important Indian chronicler Don Fernando de Alva Ixtlilxóchitl (called Black Flower or Vanilla Face, 1568–1648) there is a description of the difficulties which a king encountered on his search for the right bride. The Chichimecs of Texcoco allied themselves by marriages and in various ways with the stronger Aztecs, so as to retain a measure of autonomy. Nezahualcoyotl, Fasting Coyote, reigned from 1431 to 1472 over the city state. In the following report by Ixtlilxóchitl the melancholy, and always idealized, poet-king is shown from another, a quite human side.

It is the story of the marriage of Fasting Coyote (Nezahualcoyotl) with Ants' Flower (Azcalxochitzin).

The castle of the king of Texcoco, built of stones so beautifully that it did not seem to be the work of human hands, contained, besides numerous smaller rooms, a large hall where the king used to receive the rulers of Tenochtitlán, Tlacopan and other regions. In their honour, dances and other entertainments were arranged in the courtyard in front of this hall. The most notable room in the castle itself was the king's bedroom, which was circular in plan. At that time Nezahualcoyotl had not yet chosen—as was the custom of his fathers—a principal wife who should bear him his successor. He had, however, a considerable number of sons, but all of them were the children of his concubines. As respected leaders, they carried out important tasks in wars and in warlike expeditions. But the years passed and Nezahualcoyotl made no choice of a wife. His uncle, King Izcoatl (Obsidian Serpent, 1428–1440) and the latter's successor Moctezuma I (The Angry Lord, 1440–1469) no longer dared to make fresh suggestions to him, since he had once refused twenty-five maidens whom they had sent to him so that he might choose a wife from among them. At last the king himself decided to put an end to this situation. He gave orders that several girls should be brought to him, all descended from the most highly esteemed and oldest ruling families. His ancestors, the princes of the Chichimecs, had chosen their wives from among these families. Only one of the girls met with the king's approval. She came from Coatlicán, the "serpent house." As she was still very young, he gave her to his brother,

Soaring Eagle (Cuauhtlihuanitl) with the request that he should bring up the noble maiden in his house. When the girl became mature enough, she was to be brought to Nezahualcoyotl so that he could make her his wife.

Old Soaring Eagle died soon afterwards and his son inherited the house, offices and much more. When he saw the young girl, who was destined for Fasting Coyote, he married her, not knowing that she was to have been the bride of the king of Texcoco.

When, some time later, Fasting Coyote sent for the young girl, his nephew, the son of Soaring Eagle, was horrified. He answered that the maiden was already his wife; he had married her in ignorance of the agreement between the king and his father. But he was prepared to accept any punishment. When the king heard this he was angry, and handed the young man over to the judges; not finding that the accused had done anything wrong according to law, the judges set him free.

Fasting Coyote, who had hitherto been most fortunate with anything he undertook, realized that, so far as love was concerned, he was dogged by misfortune. Alone, a prey to the melancholy of his solitary heart, he went out to visit his gardens which were set in a lake. Yet there, too, he found no peace, and wandered on until he came to the "spot above the rocks." When Cuacuauhtzin, Great Eagle, saw him, he invited him to his palace. The latter was one of the fourteen great princes of the League of Cities. To give pleasure to his sovereign he arranged that his cousin, the lovely Ants' Flower, should serve him. She was still little more than a child. She had been given to Great Eagle by his uncle, to be brought up in his palace; and later, when she had grown up, he was to make her his wife. But Great Eagle had not yet touched her.

When the king of Texcoco saw the maiden, his melancholy left him, and he fell in love. He hid his feelings from his host and rushed back to the court. Very secretly Fasting Coyote made arrangements to do away with Cuacuauhtzin. He sent one of his servants, in whom he had great confidence, to the council of Tlaxcalan, and instructed him to say that on account of certain offences the welfare of the empire demanded that Cuacuauhtzin, one of the nobles, must die. He, therefore, requested the council to order the captains to kill him in the next battle, in the "floral war."[36] Simultaneously he ordered his own captains to take Great Eagle, whom he would make their commander-in-chief, to where the battle was fiercest, against the warriors of Tlaxcalan. Though Great Eagle had failed badly, the king wanted to grant him an honourable death on the battlefield.

Cuacuauhtzin was surprised to be made commander-in-chief of the Mexican troops. He knew all too well that he was too old and not at all fit to lead in such a battle. Yet he obeyed. With some poems of lament, which he had composed himself and recited at a banquet, he took his leave and went to fight the Tlaxcaltecs. As arranged and anticipated he was cut to pieces by the warriors of the enemy.

After the removal of his rival, the king of Texcoco encountered new difficulties. He was impatient to find out what the girl thought, but so that no one should know his intention. He sent a message to his sister, saying that he now was thinking of taking a wife and that Ants' Flower, who was to have become the wife of Great Eagle, appeared to him to be worthy. But as Great Eagle had died in battle only a few days earlier, it seemed to him not decent to discuss this publicly.

The king's sister knew what to do. An old servant, who visited Ants' Flower regularly to dress her hair, was instructed to tell Ants' Flower of the great esteem in which Fasting Coyote held her, and of his desire to make her his wife. The servant, further, was to tell her that the king understood how sad she must be to have lost her betrothed, but that she, on her side, ought to understand his wish and send him an answer secretly.

The answer was: "His majesty may do with her as he desires, as it is her duty to honour and to respect him."

An "informal first meeting" was arranged. The king invited her to his house. He discussed with the nobility of the empire whether it would meet with their approval if he married Ants' Flower, who was a virgin and of noble descent. The plan was unanimously approved and the wedding was celebrated with great solemnity.

With this treachery Fasting Coyote won his principal wife, and no suspicion ever arose that he might have intentionally removed Great Eagle, his rival. But those who knew his secret passed on the story of Fasting Coyote's passion and the murder it induced him to commit—an act unlike any other in the life of a king who was apparently honourable otherwise.

Tenochtitlán, the Aztecs' capital, was the main centre of religious worship and of trade and the seat of the most powerful dynasty. It was, however, at no time the capital of a united empire, as for example was Cuzco in old Peru. Texcoco, the home of Nezahualcoyotl, had a different role. This town on the opposite bank of the lake was the centre of culture, home of philosophers, scholars and poets, and the site of the largest library. The Nahuatl of Texcoco was thought to be the noblest language. Its rulers have handed their names down to posterity in a more peaceful context. It was Nezahualcoyotl who had a dam built across the lake, thereby separating the salt water from the fresh water. It was he also who puzzled about the multiplicity of gods, and was anxious to find a monotheistic religion. He left behind him the most important and best known songs of the pre-Spanish era; his people called him "the poet-prince." It is therefore all the more surprising to hear a story told of him—told even by one of his descendants—a story, human indeed but morally, to say the least, objectionable. Among the Aztecs, official historiography would have nipped such a tale in the bud; but with the free and more philosophical Chichimecs of Texcoco it could be preserved for future generations.

The Aztecs succeeded only a few years before the landing of Cortés in assuming power in Texcoco. This was due to a woman's promiscuousness. Nezahualpilli, the son of Fasting Coyote, was married, certainly out of political considerations, to a sister of Moctezuma II, who—if one can believe the chroniclers Torquemada, Clavigero and Ixtlilxóchitl—granted her favours to numerous young men. In consequence, when her husband heard of this in 1498, he had her put to death. The ruler of Tenochtitlán resented the killing of his sister. Though this did not yet lead to an open war between the two allied city states, related through various marriages, yet the influence of Texcoco was undermined and the Aztecs of Tenochtitlán acquired supremacy in the confederation of the three cities.

The Mayas

As happens often in the history of ancient times, little is reported with regard to the conditions of everyday life. To find out anything at all about this, one has to peep through the few chinks in the doors of the rulers' palaces left open for us by the chroniclers. Nothing, however, is known of the wives of the Maya rulers of the classical period. Should it ever be possible to decipher the hieroglyphs of this enigmatical civilization, the name of one or other of these princesses might be added to the books on South American history. The prospect of this is not, however, very hopeful.

It is different with regard to the post-classical period (approximately 1000–1540). The priest-princes were replaced by rulers whose interest was no longer in the stars, but in the landed property of their neighbors' daughters. The first two hundred years of that epoch (1007–1194, or according to other sources 987–1185) were a time of peace, that is, if we can rely on the prophetic books of the Chilam Balam, the Jaguar Priests, which were written down shortly after the conquest and are based on oral tradition. This period, when warriors had little to occupy them, came to a sudden end when Chac Yib Chac, the ruler of Chichén Itzá, carried away by force the bride of Ah Ulil, the chief of Izamal; this took place, furthermore, during the wedding festivities. For the history of the Mayas this act of violence, with a woman as the victim, had heavy consequences, similar to those for the Trojans after Helen was forcibly carried away to Troy. Both the bridegroom and the guests were outraged. Diplomatic mediation was unavailing. The "League of Mayapán," a confederation of the three most powerful city states of Yucatán, came to an inglorious end. Hunac Ceel, also called Cauich, the ruler of Mayapán, who originally had been closely allied to Chichén Itzá, turned his back upon Chac Yib Chac and allied himself to Ah Ulil. The background of Hunac Ceel, the central figure at the turning point of Maya history, is interesting in the light of this event, which took place around the year 1200.

It was customary on certain festive days to sacrifice to the rain god in the cenote (well) of Chichén Itzá. In the early hours of the morning, several men jumped (or were thrown) into the well. At about noon those who had survived—or at least one of them—would be hoisted up again out of the well to make known the message of the gods. On the day to which this story refers, everyone drowned. Here began the political career of Hunac Ceel, a man of sufficient courage to fashion his own fate. This is recorded in the book of the Jaguar Priests of Chumayel as follows: "It was Cauich, Hunac Ceel Cauich was the name of the man, who bowed his head over the opening at the south side of the well. Then he jumped in. Then he came out to make known the prophecies ... Then they started to make him their ruler. Then they set him on the seat of the rulers ... Previously he was not ruler."

His subordinate was the abductor of the bride, Chac Yib Chac, who was made ruler in Chichén Itzá after Hunac Ceel's plunge into the well. It may seem somewhat surprising that the ruler of Mayapán took sides not with him, but with the man who had been robbed, and that he went to war along with this ruler of Izamal against Chichén Itzá, his close ally, whose loyalty he could not doubt. Did he intend in this way to forestall by double dealing a potential threat on the part of the two towns, Chichén and Izamal? We do not know. Chac Yib Chac had not much time left to ponder as to why his master had turned against him. He was trampled to death. Nor did the ruler of Izamal enjoy for any length of time the favour of the favourite of the rain gods, Hunac Ceel. In any case, the abduction of the bride opened the way for the elimination of Hunac Ceel's rivals. A laconic report mentions that Ah Ulil was handed over as a tributary offering to "feed and nourish Hapay Can." Hapay Can, Sucking Snake, is the name of a Maya god. As human sacrifices fed the gods, this means that Izamal, being defeated, had to provide food for the gods so as to safeguard their favour with the victors. But a difficult time was beginning for the victors also. The series of fratricidal wars triggered by this incident weakened the Maya people. They found no peace for the next three centuries; and it was the Spanish conquistadores who benefitted from this.

Evidence of Matriarchal Succession

With the Mayas in Yucatán woman's status did not rule out the possibility of her becoming regent. She even was legally entitled after the death of her husband to educate her own children, who were claimants for positions of importance. In the regions ruled by the Aztecs, where patriarchy was dominant, this would have been impossible. Although statements concerning the matriarchy, which apparently was established in the Antilles and in the southern hemisphere, are extremely rare and sporadic, all chroniclers who mention it agree that it existed (without realizing its importance); it seems therefore that their statements can be accepted.

The most reliable information comes from Cieza de León, one of the few soldiers to use a pen. Arriving from Spain, he landed in Panama, and, with his eyes always open, and anxious to learn anything new, by slow stages reached Cuzco, the capital of the Incas. His notes indicate that matriarchy prevailed among the chiefs and princes on the Pacific coast. With regard to Panama he mentions twice that in the small principalities inheritance followed the female line.[37]

The Colombian nobility too, in contrast to the common people, were observers of the matriarchal principle. The position of the *zipa* (chief) always descended to the eldest son of the sister. Those sovereigns of the small kingdom of the Muiscas on the table-land of Bogotá could, in the display of their courts and the authority they enjoyed in their realms, vie with the Incas and the Aztecs. The harems of these "god-like" princes were kept supplied with prisoners of war, with young girls who had been purchased, or with maidens whom the *zipas*' own subjects were ordered to give up to them. They sometimes had more than a hundred concubines.

Beginning in Colombia, the laws against incest, which were customarily imposed elsewhere, underwent considerable changes. Cieza wrote of the chiefs of Cali in the Cauca Valley: "They marry their nieces ... and sisters," and he reported of the Island of Puná in Ecuador: "They sleep with their own sisters;" and he, a soldier, spoke indignantly of the district of Cuzco, where, he said, "they married their own nieces or sisters." His compatriot Gómara agreed, and added: "But they are soldiers."38

The army was not a professional one, but consisted only of officers, the *curaca*. These were captains who volunteered, or who were compelled against their will, to fit themselves into the imperial hierarchy; as one special privilege among others, they received from the ruler's hand a wife of imperial descent, or were, if they so desired (this is probably the meaning of Gómara's report), given in marriage in Cuzco by the Inca himself. One has to stress that the name of "sister" certainly implied a blood relationship which was, however, too narrowly interpreted by the first Europeans who came in touch with the Indians.

The Incas

Most chroniclers agree that there were in the empire of the Incas twelve rulers with their sister-wives. Finally two mutually hostile brothers, Huáscar and Atahualpa, fought each other for the empire. The winners of this fight for power were the Spaniards who landed on the coast of Peru in 1532.

Most of the legends which formed part of the Inca ideology claim Inti, the sun god, as divine ancestor of the dynasty which later on was to become so successful. Manco Capac, one of the sons, and Mama Ocllo, one of Inti's daughters, became the first god-like, still semi-mythological rulers of the dynasty. According to other Spanish sources of the early colonial time, the rulers traced back their family tree to four brothers, who had been sent down to earth together with their four sisters by the creator god. It is possible that these four had originally been historic tribal chiefs, who, having gained mighty allies through marriage, were able to secure for themselves and their realms considerably enlarged territories. From about 1350 to 1532, a short but not unimportant period, these "Sons and Daughters of the Sun" ruled, always in couples, over old Peru.

The sister-wife of the Inca was called *coya* (queen); her outstanding importance arose at first through her relationship to her family, and was later due to her gradually acquired prestige in the continuance of the reigning dynasty. Marriage with the sister was originally not compulsory; the Inca married his own sister only when his political power had already been safeguarded by family ties. The privilege of marrying a sister was his alone. No one else was allowed to marry a relation of the first degree: "I, the Inca, herewith command that nobody may marry his sister, mother, cousin, aunt, niece, or relation, or the godmother of his child, on pain of losing both eyes." This is reported in the chronicle of Poma de Ayala, which adds: "The Inca alone is allowed to marry his own sister."

With this law, the Incas safeguarded their inviolable claim to divine descent. Only the pure-blooded sons of the *coya* could aspire to become successors to the throne. It is difficult to prove that in practice this restriction was actually observed, since the historical tradition sanctioned by the state would tend to eliminate discrepancies and imperfections. Cieza de León states that the future emperor could marry only the legitimate daughter of his parents, but states that there was a certain degree of divergence from this regulation. If the sister-wife had, or later bore, a son by another man, that son inherited the throne without regard to any of the sons whom the ruler might otherwise have.39

Moreover, no princess or relative of the imperial family was allowed to become the wife or concubine of any man of lower rank, not even if he was raised to nobility by merit.

The description which the earliest Spaniards give us of the empress of the largest empire of old America, is more definite than they could give of any Aztec queen, who was kept hidden from them. The chronicler Poma de Ayala, who himself was of Indian descent, left us in his *Nueva Corónica* portraits of the empresses who succeeded each other on the throne of Cuzco. There are in his collection beautiful and ugly empresses, happy, sad and charitable ones, some frail in health, some fond of flowers, some of birds. Some were obliging and enjoyed feasts and good food; and while one had some of the characteristics of a magician, he characterizes another as addicted to strong drink.

The clothing of the empress consisted of a tunic, blue, pink, yellow or orange in colour, which came down to the ankles, and of a vermillion sash wound round the waist. The shoulders were covered by a short cape, sometimes made of the feathers of exotic birds, and held together with a golden pin. Sandals of fine vicuña skin protected her feet; a shawl of thin wool fastened to the hair and falling loosely back over the shoulders completed her outfit. In fact, it was the same attire as that of the ordinary woman, except that it was made of more costly material. The beauty treatment used by the nobility was, however, very different from that of the common people. The ladies of the élite plucked their eyebrows with neat little tweezers, and dyed their skin with cinnabar from the mines of Huancavelicia or with the pigment of the *achiote*, a red berry. The ladies took great pains with their hair, as did the simplest peasant women. The hair was worn parted in the middle, or in tresses, and was combed repeatedly during the day with a comb made of thorns jammed into a split bamboo cane. In Peru and Bolivia, Indian women use such combs today. Artistically tied coloured threads held the entire coiffure together. The hair was washed with water in which certain barks and beans had been soaked, and mysterious herbs gave it a blue-black colour and a silken sheen.

When the exequies of a dead Inca had been performed, the new Inca assumed authority. On the same day, in the sun temple of Cuzco, the ceremony of his wedding with his sister took place, a wedding rather to be called his union with the sun, whom the *coya* symbolized. The Inca went with a great retinue to the house of the maiden. The streets through which he proceeded were spread with precious woven cloth. When he arrived at her house, the bride threw herself at his feet. Her future husband lifted her up, caused costly garments to be given to her, and asked her to put them on. Then he took a sandal embroidered with gold and put it on her right foot. This ceremony, though less elaborate, took place also among the lower orders of the population. Then he offered her, as a dowry, one hundred women servants, who either belonged to noble families or had been chosen as children of six to eight by the officials of the Inca, and who had, until that day, lived in the temples or so-called convents. The Spaniards called them "sun maidens." The Inca then gave his hand to his wife and invited her to proceed to the temple of the Sun. There the high priest was waiting for the couple, and offered them two cups of chicha, which were poured out as a libation to the gods. Next two white llamas were slaughtered.

These festivities lasted for as much as three months, and all dignitaries of the state, even ambassadors who had to journey more than a thousand miles, were present. Besides the religious ceremonies, numerous ritual dances were performed, and plays may have been enacted.

In the ritual dances performed by the nobles, women played a part. When, to enhance the festival, the family of the highest Inca danced the *way-yaya* in the large square of Cuzco, to the dull accompaniment of drums, the dancers formed two rows, one consisting of men and the other of women. The members of the very high nobility danced also in groups of three, one man holding a noble lady with each of his hands and making them whirl without stopping.

Besides the fulfilment of religious duties, the tasks of the empress and of the ladies of the first nobility consisted in weaving and in the sewing of precious garments for the Inca.

The principal wife of the Inca was not, like the wives of the Aztec rulers, without influence on state policies. At the time of the Spanish conquest the people still remembered very well how the sister-wife of the Inca Pachacutec, when he was travelling elsewhere, had organized all the work of salvage and supply after a heavy earthquake had destroyed the town of Arequipa. When, however, the husband was present and a dispute arose between him and his wife, she always remained subservient and threw herself at his feet, remaining in this position until her husband's anger had cooled and he told her to rise.[40]

Marriage was indissoluble. The obligation of the empress to her husband lasted to the end of his life, and not infrequently she chose of her own free will to follow him in death.

The only Inca drama that has come down to us is called "Ollantay." Its theme is the passionate love of a chief for a princess—hopelessly thwarted by law. Recorded in writing in the colonial epoch, it reflects the feelings and thoughts of the people during the period of the Inca domination.

The plot is laid at an historical place, Ollantaytambo, thirty-eight kilometres from Cuzco. Ollantay, one of the bravest generals, has tragically fallen in love with "Star of Joy," the daughter of the highest Inca. He confesses this to his servant Piqui Chaqui (Gay Young Spark). At the beginning of the play they are wandering through the streets of Cuzco.

Ollantay:

"Piqui Chaqui, you come from her house. Did you see my Cusi Coyllur?" [Star of Joy]

Piqui Chaqui:

"May the Sun God protect me! Do you not know that this is forbidden? Do you not fear the wrath of the King? Is she not the Inca's daughter?"

This introduction hints at the punishment which Ollantay must expect. The Inca rejects the suitor, suggests to him that he obey the old hallowed laws, and banishes Cusi Coyllur to a convent, too late, however, as the play goes on to show. Ollantay, having returned to his home, starts a revolt.

Ollantay:

"From today, my dear Cuzco,
I shall call you my enemy.
Your warm chest will feel my heel,
I shall tear out your heart,
Give it to feed
the vultures and condors.
The great Inca is a liar,
A traitor and impostor ...
Over the hills of Sacsahuaman,[41]
The clouds my well-protected marksmen
will gather;

Fire will lick the roofs
And your blood will choke you."

The war over the princess starts when the Inca is informed that his daughter Cusi Coyllur has given birth to a child, Ima Sumac (How Beautiful). The daughter is imprisoned in an underground vault, and the furious Inca Pachacutic sends his most renowned general, Rumiñani (Stone Eye) against Ollantay. Rumiñani falls into an ambush and is overcome. He escapes alive, but has to await execution in Cuzco. Fate, however, takes another course: when Rumiñani returns defeated he finds that the Inca has died.

To re-establish his lost honour, Rumiñani offers to Túpac Yupanqui, the new Inca, to overcome Ollantay by treachery. He wounds himself, pretends to be a fugitive and is welcomed by Ollantay. This is a suitable occasion for a festivity. When Ollantay's men are drunk, Rumiñani overcomes his adversary, binds him and takes him to Cuzco.

Túpac Yupanqui, the Inca, turns to the high priest:
"What punishment do these rebels deserve?"

The general asks for the death sentence, the priest advises mercy. The ruler, who knows of Ollantay's love, pardons him and sets Cusi Coyllur free, with her child. The happy lovers fall into each other's arms, and the Inca says the final words to the audience:

"Pain and sorrow may they be ended,
My blessing to your happiness.
Your wife rests on your heart,
Light shines in the night of death."[42]

Owing to its dramatic composition and the clearly drawn characters the play is very impressive. Rumiñani is a brutal, sly and cruel soldier. Piqui Chaqui is timid, somewhat crafty, Ollantay is blinded by his passion, but without characteristic features. From a critical point of view he is the weakest, but at the same time the most sympathetic male character, and Cusi Coyllur is the great heroine, sacrificing herself, faultless.

BURIAL SACRIFICES

We owe much of our knowledge of the most ancient civilizations of the American continent to the Indian's custom of burying various possessions and offerings with the dead. In the higher civilizations, burial practices became more elaborate and were sometimes known to be associated, as in the case of the Inca rulers, with actual worship of the dead.

All of the Indian's burial practices were based on a belief in life after death. Whatever different peoples may have thought about death, there was always some kind of idea as to what the deceased might expect after he died. Usually a special place was imagined where the dead would continue to exist in a manner somewhat similar to that of their earthly life. Nearly all peoples buried their dead according to conceptions which corresponded to their way of life when on earth. The rulers were often provided in their graves with their wives and a number of slaves, not to mention clothes, food, weapons, tools and whatever else makes life more pleasant, all this to be taken with them on their journey to the other world. There was a great variety of burial places and customs. The Aztecs, for instance, cremated their dead, while in the Sinú district (Colombia) special houses were built for the corpses. In the necropolis on the uninhabited peninsula of Paracas, there were, as early as two thousand years ago, twenty to fifty families buried in crouching positions, wrapped in precious shrouds and supplied with jewelry (Ill. 112).

The different conceptions of life in the next world were largely founded on earthly social systems of class and rank. Nobles and chiefs were entitled to a continuation of the privileges they had enjoyed on earth. The common people were either denied immortality or were supposed to have a future lot similar to their earthly one.

The practice of killing human beings so as to honour the dead was customary especially in high civilizations, owing to the ideas held as to life after death. Numerous sun maidens were immolated when an Inca had died—some of the chroniclers speak of more than a hundred. Many women shaved their heads bare, blackened their faces with soot and, whipping themselves, ran with loud laments through the streets of the capital, Cuzco. The dead rulers and their wives were mummified, clad in sumptuous garments and each tied up in a bundle. Some were fitted with an "image head"—an artificial face—to make them look more lifelike. At certain festivals the Inca appeared accompanied by his ancestors, who were worshipped as gods. For the celebrations of these days, the mummies were brought from their temples and carried, accompanied by loudly lamenting women and dignitaries, through the streets of the town. This was to prove that the rulers were eternally present.

The dead Chibcha rulers were buried in hidden graves, where they lay, surrounded by the corpses of their women and servants who had been killed in their honour, and well provided with jugs filled with chicha and sacks of cocoa beans. All over the continent it was the man who had the right to claim wives, concubines and female servants for the continuation of his life after death. Exceptions confirm this rule. A Jesuit father reported that among the Natchez, another almost extinct people who once had lived in the lower Mississippi Valley, a female "Sun" died in 1704. Her husband was not a member of the nobility but of the low rank of the "stinkards." When his wife died he was strangled, so that he could accompany her to the "great village of the dead."

GODDESSES OF ANCIENT AMERICA

In the Indian mind, the myth of creation was related closely to man. According to the legend of creation of the Quiché Mayas, who lived in the highlands of Guatemala, the gods created man, after two unsuccessful attempts, in order "to create their supporter and maintainer."

"Let us try once more,
 The time for sowing is near!
 Let us make man
 Who feeds and supports us.
 For
 What else can we do,
 That we may be invoked,
 That we may not be forgotten on earth."[43]

In the heaven of the Indian deities there are no gods symbolizing the conceptions of human reason or of human love in the Christian sense. Their heaven reflects the needs of earth, is a mirror of the hierarchy of the living. The gods are not loved and feared, but only feared and placated. They are demons, representing the forces of nature to whose unrestrained discretion man is mercilessly subjected.

Mexico

The Aztecs thought they were living in the epoch of the "Fifth Sun." The previous four worlds had been destroyed by the gods. The Fifth Sun, being under the symbol *olin* (movement), was to meet its end through a tremendous earthquake.

The cycle of nights and days was attributed to the activity of a monster-goddess who devoured the sun each night and, if it pleased her to do so, brought it to life in the morning. The reappearance of the sun was never to be taken for granted.

It is easy to understand how the fear of the disappearance of the sun (comparable with today's fear of destruction by atomic energy) would be expressed in religious dogma and become the motive for a cult that was frequently cruel. Gods conceived of in this way could be appeased by man only with the most precious of his possessions: human blood and human hearts were offered to sustain the gods and save man from ruin.

COATLICUE

In Tenochtitlán, the Indians built a temple which they called "House of Darkness." It was dedicated to the

Tlazoltéotl, the goddess of the earth and vegetation, the goddess of filth

Aztec goddess Coatlicue, the "Filth-eater," goddess of love and, at the same time, of sin. It was she who created all life, and simultaneously she who devoured all life. Whatever she did, she was in the cold grip of death (Ill. 66). To look at her image is terrifying; hidden in her is the secret of a strange world. Coatlicue, the "Goddess with the skirt of snakes," was not a woman, she was the personification of awesome natural forces, the original symbol of the ambivalence of all human life.

As mother of Huitzilopochtli, the Aztec god of war, she personifies earth, opposed to heaven, which was personified by a solar god. She was the monster who devoured the sun at night and brought it to life again in the morning.

The artist did not see her as a humanized being but as the unity of opposites. Out of a small human kernel there grow rampantly in all directions animal qualities, those of beasts of prey. The centre alone is a female torso with slack, drained breasts. She is not a young goddess like, for example, Xochiquetzal. Coatlicue is ageless. Down from the hips she wears a skirt made of the entwined bodies of snakes, round her neck a necklace, reaching down to the navel, formed of human hearts and hands. Her breastplate is a skull. The slightly raised, deformed arms resemble the jaws of snakes, preparing to attack. Her legs are jaguar claws. Two interlaced heads of snakes form her head; they are arranged symmetrically, their long and forked tongues hanging out of their mouths. Touching each other, they show in front and behind the forked tongues of reptiles. Eduard Seler,[44] the German Americanist (1849–1922), saw in the two heads of snakes the symbol of two streams of blood issuing from the decapitated body of the goddess. Seler thinks that the conception of showing the goddess of earth decapitated stems from Aztec rites; according to tradition, in the course of feasts celebrated in the honour of the goddess, a woman representing Coatlicue was decapitated and then flayed. The flaying, the stripping off the skin of the sacrificial victims who represented the gods, was the symbol of the rejuvenation of nature. These vegetation rites were performed every spring.

It is interesting that a relief is incised under the base of the sculpture, representing a deity of vegetation (Tlaloc). This detail added by the artist was not visible to the observer. As it formed a substantial part of his story, it should not be omitted, otherwise his "prayer in stone" would have lost its magical power. He was not concerned to show everything to the living. More conservative representations show Coatlicue with a skull as head (Ill. 71).

Coatlicue was the strangest goddess of pre-Spanish America. She probably was among the most ancient of the deities. The metaphysical conceptions of death and resurrection, which came together in her as the "Filth-eater," belong to the oldest ideas of mankind. This type, however, of the Aztec earth goddess was characteristically Indian, and therefore, more than almost any other female figure, she provides the key to the understanding of this very remote world. A temple was erected for her as Tonanzin (Our Mother), on the site of which there stands today the church of the "Virgen de Guadalupe," the patron-saint of the Mexican Indians.

In Mesoamerica the belief was widespread that the earth was a flat disc, lying on the back of a crocodile or—corresponding to the four quarters of the compass—on the backs of four crocodiles swimming in the primeval sea. The heavens therefore supported the four Chacs (rain gods in the language of the Mayas). A myth of the Nahua tribes about creation tells of a large female monster with innumerable mouths, swimming in the shapeless masses of water of this sea, and devouring everything it could get hold of. When the two gods Quetzalcóatl (Feathered Serpent), and Tezcatlipoca (Smoking Mirror), saw it, they decided to give a solid shape to the earth. They transformed themselves into snakes, and attacked the monster from both sides to destroy it. The lower part of the monster was transformed into the sky, while the upper one sank down and became the earth. The snake symbolized not only fertility and the female principle, but it was also the beginning and the end, the symbol of time, which the Indian could not consider apart from space. This monster, called Cipactli, underwent still further change, until it matured into the image of Coatlicue. As goddess or monster, she was threatening and at the same time beneficent, the purifying element, which was to liberate men and gods from their "sins." This strange idea of a decapitated earth goddess is connected with the myth of her origin:

When her adversaries had mutilated Coatlicue—says the myth—her hair turned to grass, to trees, to flowers. Her skin was transformed into fertile soil, her eyes to holes filled with water, wells and springs. Her mouth changed into great caves, which offered shelter to men.

Out of her nose were formed hills and valleys. She it was who secured life with her sacrifices.

When the "Goddess with the snake skirt" cried at night, she could only be consoled with human hearts. As long as she was refused these, she brought no peace and gave no fruit. She had to be sprinkled with human blood, a notion which had its greatest hold in the densely populated districts of the Aztecs, Chichimecs and Tlaxcaltecs. (The economic background of human sacrifices has been described above.)

CHALCHIUHTLICUE

As we search for the origin of the gods, we at the same time uncover the history of mankind. "They called the place Teotihuacán because it was the burial place of the kings, and the Old say of them, he who is dead has become a god. Therefore when one says of someone that he has now become a *téotl* (god), this means that he is dead."

These few lines were all that the early Spanish chroniclers found to say about the most marvellous town in ancient Mexico, which was larger than Athens, larger than Rome. Recent excavations indicate that it was destroyed by fire. Strictly speaking, Teotihuacán was the religious capital, in a wider sense the birthplace of the gods.

The two largest buildings, known as the "pyramids of the sun and of the moon" (Ill. 62), were probably connected with the rain god Tlaloc (He who makes grow), his female counterpart, the water goddess Chalchiuhtlicue (the Lady with the skirt of jade) (Ill. 63). The inhabitants of the highlands often connected her with the moon. In a myth of creation she represented, as wife of Tlaloc, the connection with heaven, so very important for man. In various religious conceptions she is identical with the goddess Coatlicue. According to legend she sent a flood on the earth and transformed men into fishes. In later times she occupied a place under the nine rulers of the night. According to the Codex Fejérváry-Mayer, it was the water goddess who gave too much moisture to the young maize plant so that it began to rot. At first the young plant had to fight with the earth's crust which was symbolized by Tepayollotli, the ruler of the inner forces of the world. In this fight to break through the earth crust the rain god Tlaloc helped her. Moderate rain was necessary; too much or too little were disastrous, and the scorching sun was fatal. Thus, the gods symbolized nature, upon which prosperity or ruin depends, and for which man at that time had only a partial explanation or none at all.

CHICOMECÓATL

The goddess Chicomecóatl, "Seven Snake," was an important deity. She held the post of maize goddess in the heaven of the Aztecs. Probably she was incorporated in the Aztec heaven so as not to offend any subjected or allied tribes who venerated her. In the northwest of Mexico among the tribes of the Tarascans she was worshipped under the name of Cueraváperi, the sister-wife of Curicaveri, who like his Aztec cousins was connected with the elements of the sun and of fire.

Human sacrifices were made to Chicomecóatl during a feast called *ochpaniztli*. Like all Mexican deities this beneficent goddess had negative qualities, too: famines, for example, were ascribed to her. During the feast of *tlaxochimaco*, songs were sung in her honour; this is one of them, transmitted by Sahagún:

"[Goddess] of the Seven Cobs
Rise,
Awake, for
You, Our Mother,
Are leaving us now,
Going back to your home
Tlalocan [the country of rains]."

This song was repeated in innumerable verses. It was the duty of the goddess to awake the slumbering vegetation, to stimulate the young maize plant to spring up and to grow.

TLAZOLTÉOTL

Tlazoltéotl, called the Goddess of Filth—that is, of sin—was the earth and vegetation goddess of the Huaxtecs on the Gulf coast, later worshipped in the highlands as well. She was particularly honoured as the mother of the young maize gods, the male Cintéotl and the female Xilonen (Ill. 70). In her Mexican form she had four aspects related to the four phases of the moon. To her third aspect belonged the power to cleanse, blotting out all sins. As her name indicates, she represented forces associated with the idea of the unclean, and was commonly used by the Aztecs to denote sexual excesses. Her priests heard the confession of those found guilty of adultery. She had female priestesses and assistants. Phallic dances were performed in her honour. She was thought to be connected with witchcraft as well.

Gods help the young maize plant to pierce the crust of the earth
(from the Codex Fejérváry-Mayer)

XOCHIQUETZAL

Xochiquetzal, the "Precious One" or the "Upright standing Flower," was the goddess of the earth's fertile crust and of flowers. She was at the same time patron of sexual love, and was associated, in another aspect, with all types of handicrafts. She is remembered chiefly as the goddess of love and beauty, who lived on the top of a mountain surrounded by dwarfs, musicians and female dancers. With her charm she even enticed the otherwise very reserved Tezcatlipoca, whose name in Nahuatl means "Smoking Mirror," who then abducted her from her divine husband Tlaloc whose principal wife she was.

  "She is a real goddess,
    So charming and gay.
    I must win her
    Not tomorrow or later;
    This is my command and thus it shall be.
    I command it, I the young warrior,
    I, the sun-like,
    Who am as beautiful as the rising sun."[45]

The everyday life of the Mexicans was enriched with flowers, songs and play, symbolized by the earthly representatives of Xochiquetzal and her twin brother Xochipilli, the flower-prince, in whose honour festivities were given. On a certain day, a bower of roses was made in front of the temple of Huitzilopochtli, who is to a large extent identical with Tezcatlipoca. Dressed as humming birds and butterflies, young people danced around the image of Xochiquetzal, Precious Flower.

A very old tradition speaks of a great flood: all men were drowned, but not the gods Xoxcox and Xochiquetzal. These two had many children, but none of them could speak or sing. Legend has it that a white dove came and gave different languages to all these dumb beings. Xochiquetzal was the first mother of twins and was honoured as the mother of the young maize god. It was believed that she brought good luck to children.

But even a song of hers, the most lovable goddess, expresses sadness.

  "From the land of the rains
    and of the mist
    I am come,
    Xochiquetzal.
    To the land of decay
    I am to go."

TOZI

When the Aztecs conquered other tribes, they not only demanded tribute from the vanquished, but also allotted to the latters' gods seats in their own heaven—bribes, as it were, for the gods' favour. They were, however, far from aiming at the establishment of a state religion, such as the one instituted by the Incas. Thus, the dull heaven of the gods hanging above Tenochtitlán was enriched by the addition of a laughing deity who had come up from the fertile district of the vanilla, the country of the Totonacs, to the cooler mountains of the highlying valley. Clay images of the goddess Tozi, "Our Grandmother" (who is sometimes referred to as Teteoin-

60

nan) with her radiant smile, the so-called *caras sonrientes*, smiling faces, are unique in their human quality. Human models may have been used; the terracottas may be likenesses of priestesses serving the goddess Xochiquetzal. In appearance the childlike figure resembles the gods of the Asian continent rather than those typical of ancient Mexico (Ill. 52, 54). From Tozi emanated a healing force. She was a friendly goddess, and the patron of steam baths.

ILAMATECUHTLI
The "Old Mistress" was a life-saving mother-goddess, certain of her features resembling those of the goddess Tozi, "Our Grandmother." Numerous small votive offerings made from rough moulds show the goddess, in the later Aztec period, with a child in her arms.

NELLITÉOTL
"The true God" or Ipalnemohuani, "He by whom we live," was "Our Father" and "Our Mother" simultaneously. It is characteristic of this deity, who was included only late in the Mexican religion, that she could at once appear as man and woman, simultaneously begetting and bearing. Unlike the Maya deities Tepeu- Gucumatz, she did not make a specific appearance when man was created. This deity stood outside space and time. She was also called Ometéotl, "Twice God" (or "Two Gods"), or Ometecuhtli, "Twice Master" (or "Two Masters"). The number "two" combines the differentiated, yet complementary, male and female forces.

CENTZON TOTOCHTIN
Centzon totochtin, "Four hundred rabbits," shows female traits, partly because of her lunar character. Her worship was developed in the most detailed manner in the Mexican confederate state of Morelos. High above Tepoztlán, on the edge of a steep rock, stand the ruins of the Aztec temple where festivities took place at harvest time with drinking bouts and sexual orgies.

CINTÉOTL
Only rarely provided with female attributes, this deity appears in pictographs (Fejérváry-Mayer) as protector or protectress of the young maize plants, where she is also shown in the shape of the water goddess Chalchiuhtlicue, as she herself is protected by the water deities.

COYOLXAUHQUI
"She with the golden bells" was the goddess of the moon and sister of Tezcatlipoca, the "Smoking Mirror," the martial, vigorous god of the north. The Aztecs worshipped her as goddess of the moon (Ill. 67).

IZCOLIUHQUI
"Split Obsidian" was the goddess of darkness. Eruptions of volcanoes and earthquakes are ascribed to her.

IZPAPALOTL
"Obsidian Butterfly" was a demonic goddess, symbolizing beauty and unknown fate. Sometimes death symbols are given her which then frequently are shown in the

make-up of her face. The butterfly was a symbol of fire and of war. In Xochimilco, Izpapalotl was worshipped as Chantico, in representations wearing the fire and water sign as headdress, and as an emblem of war.

MICTLANCIUATL

This goddess, who was also called Mictecaciuatl, was the ruler of the realm of the dead and companion of Mictlantecuhtli, the "Sovereign of the Underworld."

RELIGIOUS OBSERVANCES

Generally the worship of the gods was the duty of the men. The women played only a secondary role, yet owing to the large number of festivals, they could not altogether be dispensed with. Thus, during the feast of the "Great Night Vigils" *(uey tozoztli)*, Chicomecóatl, the maize goddess, and Cintéotl, the maize god, were honoured by a procession of young girls. They carried corn cobs to the temple of the goddess "Seven Serpent." There they sacrificed them to her. Singing and dancing were intended to propitiate the gods of vegetation.

Sahagún reports on the priestesses of Xochiquetzal: "The female assistant of the priest had to provide sacrifices which were required in the Atenchicalan temple: flowers and scented herbs, to be offered to Our Grandmother. It was the task of the priest's assistant to provide all that the women used for their sacrifices when they put on the robe (of the goddess) ... and when someone made a vow, it again was the assistant of the priest (the White Woman), who transmitted it. She censored all that happened there in Atenchicalan."

At the "Small Feast of the Lords" *(tecuilhuitontli)* it was the rites of the salt-workers that had to be observed, and to honour Uixtociuatl, the "Mistress of the Saltwater," a woman who represented her had to be sacrificed.

A special place among the eighteen great Mexican feasts was given to the "Feast of Rain" *(ochpaniztli)*, celebrated in honour of the goddesses of prosperity and of the earth. These goddesses were represented by women and maidens carrying brooms to sweep clean the "path of the gods," to clear the way for the growth of maize, etc. All this culminated in simulated fights between women, midwives and prostitutes, and, following these, in the sacrifice of a woman, who personified Tozi or Teteoinnan, the mother of the gods. For the "Feast of the Mountains" *(tepeilhuitl)* the women made small models of maize pastry, representing the mountains of the rain gods, which were eventually eaten. The sacrifice of five women and one man terminated this feast, which closed with the request for favourable periods of rain. Another feast was *tititl* during which a woman, dressed in white and symbolizing the old goddess Ilamatecuhtli, was sacrificed. The climax of the feast was a kind of carnival procession, the young people hitting the women with longish padded sacks of hide.

A TOLTEC LEGEND

Love and the sufferings of love, envy, treason, temptation and magic—all this, of which there is so much in Greek mythology, is found only rarely in the legends of the Aztecs. Their stories speak of the hero who triumphs over the cunning and the malice of his enemies. Here even a woman could overstep the rules of custom and morals, the woman as an individual. Although written accounts belong to a later period, they were based on historical events. Through generations of oral tradition the trail leads back to a half-forgotten historical event, to a surviving myth. One of these stories, handed down from one generation to the next, was still remembered by the people at the time of the Spanish conquest. Many of the names mentioned in the legend are to be found in the early chronicles written by Spaniards and Mexican Indians shortly after the conquest. The material was collected by Cäcilie Seler, wife of the Americanist Eduard Seler, at the end of the 19th century. It is the tale of "Xochitl and the invention of pulque."

"It had been prophesied to the heroic people of the Toltecs that their realm would perish even before it had existed a thousand years. Omens would herald its ruin. The depravity of the princes and of the priests and the nobles, appointed to lead the people, and the neglect of their duties towards the gods, all this was believed to be the cause of the impending disaster. When Tecpancaltzin reigned as the eighth king of the Toltecs, Papantzin, one of his princes, came to him with presents, among them a jug filled with a beverage which his daughter, the lovely Xochitl (Flower), had invented. He called it *octli* (pulque). The father persuaded the daughter to offer it herself to the king. The ruler liked the drink, but was still more impressed by the extraordinary beauty of the maiden. He could not resist his desire, and seduced young Flower. He locked her in one of his palaces and secretly had sexual intercourse with her. There she bore him a son who was called Topiltzin, Our Prince.

"The parents of Xochitl were very sorrowful about the disappearance of their daughter and searched in vain for her. Eventually they succeeded in finding and secretly speaking to her. Flower complained, and Papantzin went to the king and upbraided him with the great wrong which he had committed.

"Tecpancaltzin assured him that he would love to have Flower for his wife, but that he was already married. (Doubtless this refers to the position of the principal wife.) Moreover he had no heirs, and would recognize the son whom Xochitl had borne him as the lawful heir to the throne. This duly took place. When the queen had died he married Xochitl, and appointed Topiltzin as his heir. Thereupon the king and his people observed with horror many of the portents which had been prophesied for the end of the reign of the Toltecs: Topiltzin was born with curly hair and this hair resisted all brushing. Moreover the ruler's relatives became jealous of his illegitimate son.

"Thus began a period of minor wars. When the king went to war he gave to Xochitl the mat (the symbol of regal power); she exercised great influence over the king also in times of peace. When his son was old enough, the king left him the stool. For the first four years Topiltzin ruled wisely and justly. Then evil thoughts and desires took hold of him. The priests became his accomplices, and all bonds of propriety and shame were broken. The Toltecs, trapped in long and major wars, were unable to resist their numerous enemies. In the course of these wars Xochitl called up even the women for war service and put herself at their head. When death overcame her on the battlefield, blood streamed from her many wounds. Then the people of the brave Toltecs scattered."

Legend and historical fact are interwoven in this story. According to the *Historia de los Reynos* (traditional legends compiled by chroniclers soon after the conquest), the Toltecs had ten kings. Their priest-king Topiltzin Quetzalcóatl, who had assumed the name of the ancient deity, was the fifth ruler of the Toltecs. He was defeated in conflict with Tezcatlipoca, Smoking Mirror, and had to flee. Tezcatlipoca, the tribal deity of another, Nahuatl speaking group, had originally also been a historical person. According to the European calendar this defeat took place in the year 997.

Old traditions accuse Quetzalcóatl of having been himself to blame for his expulsion. But in a wider sense it is connected closely with the events mentioned above and another tradition of which we shall now speak.

In the course of generations, legend linked these two tribal chiefs in one myth; gradually they developed into two of the most important gods. In the new conception of the world it was no longer man and woman who represented thesis and antithesis in the military monarchy of the Aztecs, but hostile warriors. Until the arrival of the Spaniards their conflict formed the basis of Mexican religious philosophy, in which dualism was symbolized by, on the one hand, Quetzalcóatl, who spurned human sacrifices, and on the other the bloodthirsty Tezcatlipoca. Woman, that is the primeval mother, was relegated to the background. Power politics defeated common sense.

The expulsion of Quetzalcóatl, the end of the paradisical state of mankind, had been connected with the notion of sin. Here, as in the Old Testament, it was two agents which seduced man to sin: there the apple and the woman, here pulque and the woman.

According to another legend, the ageing and sick priest-king Quetzalcóatl, who hid himself because of his ugliness, was once visited by his adversary Tezcatlipoca and the latter's brother Huitzilopochtli, and they praised the white pulque as a healing drink. "When you drink it, it will intoxicate you and make your body weightless. You will weep and be sad. You will think of your death and where you then shall go." Quetzalcóatl let himself be persuaded, and drank—as had been planned—even a fifth cup, which was one cup too many. In his drunkenness the priest-king forgot the rites and sinned against the law of fasting. Then he wept and a deep melancholy took hold of him.

The first part of the *Anales de Cuautitlán* (Codex Chimalpopoca), still popular in oral tradition at the time of the conquest, exposes the sin of the priest-king Topiltzin Quetzalcóatl still more clearly. When intoxicated, he called for his sister ". . . so that we may both get drunk." He seduced his sister. They forgot the gods, thus bringing their doom upon themselves and becoming responsible also for the fate of their people.[46]

The Mayas

Only the Mayas could vie with the Aztecs in the variety of their gods and in the number of nether worlds. Mayan deities distributed gifts lavishly. They appeared at one time as men, at another as women, sometimes with the attributes of both sexes. In the representations of them which survive we rarely find them in entirely human shape. They were endowed with the characteristics of certain animals: the dog, the owl and the lamenting-bird are shown in the sculptures or on vase paintings, sometimes half man and half vulture—they formed the retinue of the gods of death. Others were connected with one of the upper worlds (the heavens). Dead or living they performed their parts, and when the number of their duties grew too large, they divided themselves. The numerous variations in their features make it today difficult to classify them, and the meaning of the variations has frequently been lost since no written record survived. There was no chronicler for the Mayas equivalent to Father Sahagún, to whom we owe so much of our knowledge of the religious concepts of the Aztecs.

IXCHEL

To the highest deities of the Mayas belonged the god Itzamná, formerly a hero of civilization, who was associated with the sun. His wife or his own female form was the goddess of birth, of feminine handicrafts and also of sexual excess. Her name was Ixchel (Our Mother), the mother of the gods. She was a moody, and apparently very old deity. She was identified with the moon. She taught women to weave, and was the patroness of weavers and midwives, and of medicine and of prophecy. She protected women at childbirth; an image of the goddess, placed under the bed of a pregnant woman, was said to help at the birth.

Ixchel symbolized, in contrast to her husband, the dark side of life. Besides her positive functions, she had negative traits. She was, for example, responsible for floods.

Sun and moon were the first beings to have sexual intercourse. They lived together with the sun's elder brother, the planet Venus, and the moon was said to have committed adultery with Venus. Today the Quiché Mayas in the highlands of Guatemala see in the moon the deity of procreation and sexual excess. She also has power over birth. She arranges the menses, alternating them with pregnancies and ruling over these with the nine-fold return of her light. By the number nine the moon goddess became in the original religion one of the "Nine Masters of the Night" who followed the "Thirteen Masters of the Day." In the "folded books" she was therefore always surrounded by symbols of death. The Cakchiqueles who live in the highlands of Guatemala, still see today in the moon the owner of the Lake of

64

Atitlan. The moon goddess certainly functioned also as some kind of water goddess.

The headdress of this goddess was formed by entwined snakes, her jewelry consisted of bones, and instead of nails she had the claws of a jaguar on her toes. Coatlicue in Mexico might be looked upon as a corresponding deity. In Yucatán, Ixchel was also called "She of the thirteen dyed locks" or "The maiden with the pin of jade" as is shown by one of the books of the Chilam Balam of the Jaguar Priests.

IX CHEBEL YAX

The young moon goddess Ix Chebel Yax shared her functions with Ixchel. Her features were similar to those of the Mexican goddesses Tlazoltéotl and Xochiquetzal. Stone phalli discovered in the excavations in Uxmal indicate that sexual rites were performed in her honour.

FERTILITY DEITIES AND SPIRITS

Bishop Diego de Landa wrote in his *Relación*: "All that these Indians do or speak of concerns maize. Indeed they make a god of it." It is all the more surprising then, that in the religion of the Mayas there is no maize goddess of any standing similar to the Mexican Chicomecóatl or Xilonen. If we look for her, we find Yum Kaax, that pure and lovable deity, the protector of young married couples and of the maize. His image fuses with that of the god of the woods, Yumil Kaxob, and also with that of the goddess Ix Kanleox ("She of the precious cover of leaves"). In *Popol Vuh*, the sacred "Book of Advice" of the Quiché Indians (see Note 43), there is an abundance of creator deities mentioned, but hardly anything about a deity of fertility. Like all important sources from ancient America, its stories were orally handed down; in the 17th century, they were copied in Latin letters and in the original language by the priest of a small village. One episode of this book may be mentioned: The maiden Xquic, who was to give birth to the two heroes Hunahpu and Xbalanque, had to prove her identity to her mother-in-law, who sent her to the barren maize field, ordering her to bring back maize. In her need she turned to Xtoh, Xcanil and Xcacou for help. (The letter X at the beginning of a proper name shows that it is the name of a woman, but also expresses special tenderness.) Xtoh was the bringer of rain, and the two others the deities concerned with maize or cocoa. They were not true goddesses, since in the mythology of the Mayas there were only a spirit of maize, one of beans, one of chili pepper, etc., living in each individual fruit as if it were the fruit's soul.

DEMONS AND UNDERWORLD DEITIES

In the *Popol Vuh* there are seven pairs of underworld deities; in the "Book of Advice" they are mentioned only in couples without being called husband and wife. To turn them into creative couples would have been senseless, as they did not create but only destroyed.

XTABAI

They were female demons of the night, but also deities of the hunt. They were of human shape, but had no flesh, and could transform themselves at will. Often they turned into Yaxche trees or they sat in tree-trunks combing their hair. Men who met them were liable to die a sudden death. In the shape of young girls they liked to entice young men into the forest. As demons in the shape of snakes they tried to bind themselves around men and to take them to the nether world, or to throw them into a "cenote" (a hole filled with water). The inhabitants of Yucatán believe still today that female demons called Xtabai populate the woods at night. [47]

MISTRESS OF THE ROPE

The strangest deity in the heaven of the Mayas, a being probably unique in the whole history of religion, was Ixtab, "Mistress of the Rope," the goddess of suicide. In the *Codex Dresdensis* she is herself shown hanged. It was recorded that with her help suicides were admitted to a paradisical upper world. "They go to a quiet, peaceful place. No one hurts them any longer. All have plenty to eat and to drink. The huge tree, called Yaxche, offers its large branches with their cool shade as a shelter where they all can repose and rest from work for ever. There, and here, life continues for all eternity, the soul, too, lasting without end. Those who have hanged themselves are carried by the goddess Ixtab to a special place, supposed to be in heaven. Often people end their lives by hanging themselves, in particular if they are troubled by great anxieties, plagues or disease. They avoid all these vicissitudes in the realm of Ixtab."

CREATION

The *Popol Vuh* also explains why the gods created woman. Tepeu and Gucumatz, the creator couple of the Quiché, met one day and decided to create man, as their "supporter and maintainer." Three endeavours were unsuccessful; only at the fourth and last were the gods more fortunate. This time they had made man of maize brought by animals from a hiding place behind the mountains. With the maize mash Tepeu and Gucumatz formed four men. These creatures were, however, so perfect that they resembled the gods. They could see into the farthest corners of the earth and therefore were godlike. But these would suffer no similar creatures alongside them. So the "Life-giving" and the "Creator of Sons" started again: "What are we to do? They are to see only what is near, not any farther! They are to see only the immediate. Otherwise would they not become [our] equals? Equal to us, whose knowledge comprehends what is far away and who can see everything." Thus they spoke to each other, Huracán ("Heart of the Heaven"), the Small Lightning, the Green Lightning, the mighty Gucumatz and Tepeu (the "Life-giving" and the "Creator of Sons"), and they tried once more to create men. The eyes of men were now breathed upon by the Heart of Heaven and thus their sight was dimmed as when one breathes upon a mirror. Only what was near, only nearness could they still see. This distressed men very much. To make them happy again, the gods gave them four women. "Then the women came into existence, appearing when the men were asleep. Truly, these women were beautiful, side by side with the Wood Jaguar, the Night Jaguar, the Master of the Night, and the Moon Jaguar. The wife of the Wood Jaguar called herself 'Water from Heaven;' the wife of the Night Jaguar called herself 'Water from the Well;' the wife of the Master of the Night was called 'Humming Bird Water' and 'Parrot Water' was the name of the wife of the Moon Jaguar. They themselves gave birth to men, the men of the small and the great tribes."[48]

Deities of the South

The further south we look, the more we find the clear conceptions of the gods obliterated. Tribes speaking Chibcha were settled between Central Ecuador and the Lake of Nicaragua, that is, between the high civilizations of Mesoamerica in the north and the central Andes in the south. Their historical home was somewhere in the Cordilleras of Colombia.

As they spread, they met in northern and eastern Colombia people of Aruacan origin, who were linguistically

related to various agricultural tribes of the low-lying valleys of the Orinoco and of the Amazon. At the time of the conquest there were three centres of higher civilizations in the Chibcha speaking territory: the petty principalities in Costa Rica and in Panama; the tribes of the Chibcha in the middle and upper Cauca Valley; and in particular the Muiscas in the highlands of Bogotá (Cudinamarca).

THE MUISCAS

During the First World War, Karl Theodor Preuss was still able to study the ancient agricultural tribe of the Cágaba (Colombia), whose religion retained many old concepts that contributed to our understanding of the lost knowledge of the religion of the Muiscas.

The Cágaba attribute creation to Gautéovan, the primeval mother, who created from her menstrual blood first the sun and later all other things. From her are derived also the spirits hostile to man, who bring sickness to animals and human beings. As with the Aztecs, Mayas, and Incas, the creator deity was in the course of time relegated to the background, worship and supreme reverence becoming concentrated on the sun god, whom the goddess Gautéovan had created. From her, the primeval mother, descended also the first four priest-kings, the ancestors of the later generations of priests, who, according to the myth, created justice and morals and gave them to mankind. Their office was hereditary. In the very earliest times they made a pact with the demons for the benefit of man. From these demons, they received faces (masks) to fight illness and to influence growth and favourable periods of rain. Religious feasts took place in circular wooden buildings, which once were called "houses of the sun."

The civilized people of the Muiscas also worshipped a "Primeval Mother," a fertility goddess with pronounced lunar traits. At the time of the conquest, Chiminigagua, the creator god, was no longer worshipped; he had yielded to the younger gods. When in the earliest times he made light shine on the lagoon near Tunja, Furachogua, "The Good Woman" (also called Bachúe), emerged from the water. She held in her arms a three-year-old boy, whom she married when he was grown-up. She had many children by him, four or six at each confinement. Together they wandered through many countries, indeed over the whole earth, and their descendants are mankind. When they had taught man to obey the commandments, they returned in their old age to the lagoon and

transformed themselves into water snakes. Men therefore thought that the lagoons were peopled by snake gods and worshipped them. Best known was the Lagoon of Guatavita, where gold, emeralds and precious garments were sacrificed to the "Good Woman." After the conquest, this worship became the origin of the legend of the "gilded man," El Dorado. The inhabitants told the Spaniards that on certain days the prince, completely covered with gold, was rowed out into the lagoon to be united to Bachúe. This also served as a religious justification of his claim to the rulership.

Besides these higher beings, the Muiscas of Colombia had a large number of gods each protecting an individual sphere. Chuchabiba, the "Rainbow," was the goddess protecting pregnant women. Nencatacoa was worshipped by female weavers. Huitaca was the goddess of dancing, drunkenness and sexual excess, an antagonist, as it were, of the gods of creation, who taught men the moral laws for the upholding of custom and decency. The Muiscas of Colombia did not have an organized priesthood, as did the Mexicans, Mayas or Incas.

THE CUEVAS

The Cuevas of the Isthmus of Darien worshipped with prayers and sacrifices the heavenly god Chicu me, who had created the world. The sex of this god has not been clearly indicated. There were two more goddesses, the thunderstorm goddess, Dobeiba, and a bad spirit, Tuyra. More clearly defined, however, among all these tribes is the cult of the ancestors, because here, as elsewhere in ancient America, the dead were conceived of as mediators between the supernatural powers and the living.

All the tribes that had settled in the region between the northern Andes and the Isthmus of Panama were divided into numerous small groups which, at various levels of civilization, were at best able to form miniature states, continually fighting each other. The most successful were the Chibcha in the highlands of Bogotá, who were on the point of founding a powerful state, when this development was interrupted by the Spanish conquest.

Peru before the Incas

Knowledge of the religion of the pre-Inca civilizations of Peru is only provided by the excavations, yet these are plentiful. Worship was already centred on a jaguar deity in the period of Chavín, about 900–200 B.C., so called with reference to Chavín de Huántar in the northern highlands, its most important place of worship.

At the time of the second Pan style, of the Tiahuanaco-Huari civilization, about A.D. 200–800, the sun was the central object of worship. In the middle of the frieze on the upper part of the sun-gate of Tiahuanaco in Bolivia it is represented with human features, surrounded by rays ending in the heads of pumas and condors.

Numerous lesser civilizations preceded the empire of the Incas, those of Paracas, Nazca, Recuay, Moche, and Chimu—to name only the most important. There, man still thought in terms of individual images and tried to arrange all that seemed inexplicable to him in a sequence of pictures. In the myths he searched for explanation, which had always to fit in with the particular surroundings involved and which was emotional rather than rational. Thus developed a world of demons, which characteristically combined human features with those of animals and plants. The result of this fusion was a multitude of mixed beings whose parts were taken from different aspects of nature. The peculiarity of this world of demons, as it is shown to us by the offerings in the graves on the northern coast, consists in the exceedingly realistic character of these imaginary beings. Among the nameless deities who, unlike the demons, have mainly human features, there is one goddess whose superhuman rank is indicated by teeth of a canine nature. She seems to have frequently assumed the role of a judge (Ill. 106).

Less realistic is the representation of the world of demons and gods of the southern coast. For some supernatural beings the artists had already developed a kind of iconography. In this supernatural world there was neither man nor woman: one can only recognize individual masculine and feminine features. In the pre-Inca civilizations, myth expressed the amazement of the primitive man who was as yet unable to explain what was happening around him.

The Incas

A varied collection of demons had developed in pre-Inca Peru, but no Olympus; the Incas made their entry on the stage when the time had become ripe to create, out of the puzzling variety of mythical conceptions, a well-thought-out order of deities.

STATE RELIGION

In the course of their empire's comparatively short reign, they succeeded, in great part through their claim to descend directly from the sun god, in bringing about a union of church and state. The various hierarchies of the numerous gods and demons of the earlier civilizations now lost importance. All religious tasks were now the duty of a priesthood organized, like the imperial officials, in classes, and under the rule of the high priest Villachumu, who belonged to the imperial family. He was always a brother, uncle or other near relative of the emperor and thereby of the sun god. He held all the strings in his hands. It is not surprising that this thoroughly organized and powerful religion was not split into schismatic groups like those of the other civilizations in the central region of the Andes, but rather developed toward a monotheism somewhat similar to that of the Christian religion. Religion supported the state, which in return furthered religion.

POPULAR DEITIES

Yet it was not possible to extirpate completely from popular belief the ancient gods and superstitions. In Peru, Viracocha was thought to be the creator of the world and of all things.

"Viracocha, lord of the world!
  Neither man nor woman,
  In any case master of passion
  And worship."

This is the beginning of a prayer to him. If we may believe ancient sources, no sacrifices were made to him. It was said of him that "he had neither bones nor flesh like man" and he was never represented in any image. There can be no doubt that the god Viracocha was borrowed from the earlier civilizations preceding the Incas. More important for earthly affairs than the creator god were the gods of the sky, that is, the gods and goddesses of the sun, the moon, the stars and the thunder. To these were added the goddesses of the earth and of the sea. The earth goddess Pachamama was worshipped in the highlands; she was responsible for agriculture. On the coast, there was the sea goddess Mamacocha upon whom depended a good catch of fish.

MAMAQUILLA, THE MOON GODDESS

The Indians of the lower ranks, in particular those on the coast, preferred to make supplications to the moon

68

rather than to the sun. With its cool nights and the dew of the morning, it seemed to them easier to approach, more familiar and less rigid and severe than the sun. Although at the time of the Incas the sun god was the official deity, the father of the Incas and of his sister-wife, and although the most magnificent temples were built in his honour, yet all this seemed to the peasants rather uncanny, not altogether to be trusted. The moon, on the other hand, was softer, more feminine, and changed the appearance of its face more frequently. Sometimes it disappeared completely, sometimes showed itself in the form of a sickle or as a full disc; each phase had some importance. Any peasant sowing while the moon was full would have been considered careless; but, according to tradition, he was well advised who sacrificed to the moon as soon as he, "the Orange-coloured," was surrounded by a milk-white halo.

Under the Inca rule the moon goddess Mamaquilla—less frequently worshipped in the cold highlands than on the hot coast—nevertheless took an important part in the making of the calendar and the arrangement of festivals connected with it. Theories about the eclipse of the moon resembled those in many parts of the world. In Peru it was a mythical beast who tried to devour the moon goddess, a jaguar, puma or serpent, but by using force one could chase it away.

PACHACAMAC

Another religious heritage of the inhabitants of the coast was Pachacamac. One of the most famous legends speaks of an Indian woman—symbol of mother-earth—who on the one hand was the wife of the god Pachacamac, and on the other that of an animal-deity who had assumed the appearance of a jaguar. She was the mother of twins, of the sun and the moon. It was said that her husband had drowned himself in the sea and was transformed into an island. "Saddened by this misfortune," for which no reason is given, "the unfortunate widow left while night still ruled over the world, and fell a prey to the fangs of a jaguar who attacked and ravished her." The twins, however, were saved. In all this the fox played an important part; by a ruse he pushed the jaguar over a precipice, killing it. In another version of the legend, the mother of the jaguar hid the newborn twins in a pumpkin, where they stayed until they were grown up. A bird revealed the crime to the twins, whereupon the latter killed the monster. In all the ver-

sions of the legend the twins ascended to heaven. According to a very poetical version they did so by using a liana, which for that very purpose had grown up into the sky. Arrived at the firmament, they transformed themselves into benevolent stars, the sun and the moon.

But let us leave the legends and return to Pachacamac's position in history. As "Supporter of the World" he had his most important sanctuary in the temple of the same name. After the conquest by the Incas another temple dedicated to the sun god was added to it, as well as a convent for the sun maidens. Hernando Pizarro was the first European to enter the temple, as famous in Peru for its oracle as Delphi was in ancient Greece. He reports: "The town of the temple is very large and contains great buildings and spacious courtyards. Outside there is a large space, surrounded by a wall with one door leading into the temple. In this intermediate space are the houses for the women, who are said to be the wives of the devil. The store rooms, where the gold was kept, also are there. Apart from these women, nobody lives at this place. Their sanctuaries are the same as those of the sun ... Before anyone was allowed to enter the outer part of the temple, he had to fast for twenty days and still longer than that before he could go up to the highest courtyard. In the upper courtyard there was usually a priest."[49]

INTI

In addition to the worship of Viracocha and Pachacamac, the two traditional deities, the worship of the sun of course occupied the most important place in the Inca religion. Inti, the sun god, gave warmth to the people of the highlands and together with his wife, the moon goddess Mamaquilla, ruled over the firmament. It was he, as mentioned above, who was said to have been the ancestor of the Inca. This divine descent gave to the dynasty, which originated from it, the status of the "chosen people." The higher respect paid to the sun Inti as compared with that to the moon goddess Mamaquilla corresponded to the general preponderance of the male. The Inca and the sun god, his sister-wife and the moon goddess were all one for the common people, and religion taught that all weal and woe depended upon them.

SUN MAIDENS

To maintain the cult of the gods with all its pomp and its festivities required innumerable people. Some of the

Spanish chroniclers had not been able to shake off the ideas they brought with them from their homeland. Thus they interpreted the sun maidens as "nuns," and their temples as "convents;" or, reflecting a common Christian attitude of the time toward "pagan" religions, referred to the sun maidens as "women of the devil." Although the "chosen women" and the priests served all the gods, yet the sun was so predominant that well-informed chroniclers always spoke only of sun maidens and called all sanctuaries sun temples.

That those "chosen" were not the plainest and most stupid is evident. The Inca used only a few of them, at the age of thirteen or fourteen, as presents for his officers or relatives, while the majority were allotted to the "convents" of the sun maidens, where, forever remaining virgins, they had to serve in the religious cult. The sun maidens proper were interned in their institution. They worked neither for themselves nor for any other human being. They were considered to be the spouses of the sun, whom they had to serve and for whom they prepared "food and drink" (offerings). It was not easy to become a sun maiden—a hard period of probation was required for this. Moreover, the official of the Inca to whom the girls were presented had to give his consent. The points considered were the girl's looks, her intelligence and her general physique. If these were approved, her face was covered with a grey or brownish veil; her hair was cut, leaving only some plaits on the forehead and the temples. She was given a grey dress, and the priest explained to her her duties and responsibilities. The "novice" then was handed over with a group of ten girls of about twelve years of age, to an experienced woman who would initiate her. The "novitiate" lasted about three years. The curriculum contained, apart from instruction in mythology, instruction in the art of weaving, sewing, the preparation of food, the care of objects used for the cult and the maintenance of the sacred fire.

At the end of three years the priest came again and asked the novices to decide now definitely between marriage and consecration. If they chose the position of sun maidens, any violation of the regulations was punished with death by being buried alive. As a great privilege some of them—so these most unfortunate among the chosen were told—would be immolated in case of any specially grave circumstance requiring human sacrifices, such as the illness or death of the Inca or any terrible plague.

THE RETURN TO OUR MOTHER

America had been conquered by Europeans and converted by their missionaries. The Christian religion had borne fruit among the Indian population of Mesoamerica but had not established deep roots. The conquest was seen not merely as the defeat of the people; it simultaneously brought about the fall of the Indian hero gods and the end of a cosmic cycle. With the foundation of a new rule, the Indians returned in a sense to the safer, more pacific female deities. This doubtless was one of the decisive reasons for the rapid acceptance and the popularity of the worship of the Holy Virgin. The Indian took her over from the victors, yet not without giving her Indian features. He left the "Virgen de Remojadas" to the "White Gods" (the Europeans); his own "Virgen de Guadalupe" has become a creature of the Mexican soil. Was Roman Catholicism a religion forced upon the Indians? Yes and no. For the Indians one thing only was essential, that their social, human and religious relations to the surrounding world and to supernatural holy beings should be re-established. Then their individual life could again be fitted into a larger existence, a cosmic order. The goddesses of the times before Cortés' landing were mothers, deities of fertility, part of the cosmic rhythm, of vegetation and agrarian rites. The Virgin of Guadalupe, worshipped today, is also a mother. Some Indian pilgrims still call her by the name of Guadalupe-Tonanzin, "Our Mother."

NOTES

1 In the early twenties, Paul Rivet estimated the population at 40–45 millions, a number which is no longer undisputed today. The calculations published in the following years testify to the uncertainty of our knowledge. The numbers range between the extreme points of 8.4 millions (Kroeber 1939) and 90 resp. 112.5 millions (Dobyns 1966). Compared with the European population of the late Middle Ages, the number given by Paul Rivet has not lost much of its credibility.

2 Huaqueros, derived from huaca which means sanctuary, sanctified place, burial ground, etc.

3 *Historia general de las Cosas de la Nueva España*, 12 vols., ed. Mexico D.F. 1956, and *Codex Florentino*, 13 vols., published by the School of American Research and the University of Utah, Santa Fé, New Mexico 1950–63. English translation: J. C. Anderson & C. E. Dibble, Santa Fé, New Mexico 1950–63.

4 *Codex Mendoza*, copy, as the original is not extant. The Viceroy Mendoza had it explained by natives and sent the pictographic codex with Spanish notes to the Emperor Charles V. It is included with a commentary — which from a scientific point of view is no longer valid — in Kingsborough's monumental work *Antiquities of Mexico I and V*. Modern editions were published in 1925 and 1951 in Mexico D.F. A famous English edition in 3 volumes was edited by Cooper Clark, Oxford 1938. For Peru the most important traditional account by a native author is Poma de Ayala's *Nueva Corónica y buen Gobierno*, a manuscript which was found in Copenhagen in the early twentieth century and published for the first time in Paris in 1936.

5 Diego de Landa, *Relación de las cosas de Yucatán*, English translation, ed. with notes by Alfred M. Tozzer, Cambridge 1941.

6 *Libro de Chilam Balam de Chumayel*, Mexico D.F. 1952, also other editions.

7 Pedro Cieza de León, *The Incas*, ed. with an introduction by Victor Wolfgang von Hagen, University of Oklahoma, 1959.

8 Pedro Sarmiento de Gamboa, *Geschichte des Inkareiches*, ed. Richard Pietschmann, Berlin 1906.

9 Garcilaso de la Vega el Inca, *Comentarios reales que tratan del origen de los Incas*, Lisbon 1609. English translation: *The Incas: The Royal Commentaries of the Inca Garcilaso de la Vega*, ed. Alain Gheerbrant, 1959.
The second part was published in Cordoba only in 1617. In the meantime several editions appeared mostly abbreviated. The first complete edition was published in Madrid in 1723. The most recent edition appeared in the "Biblioteca de autores españoles," vols. 133 and 134, Madrid 1960.

10 The Spaniards called the nobles under the dynasty of the Incas "Big Ears" (Orejones), because the dignity of the wearer was measured by the size of the earplugs they used to wear; the plugs made the ears appear larger.

11 Mesoamerica: Geographical designation for regions between North Mexico and the southern parts of Nicaragua and Panama. This comprises the regions south of the Mexican rivers Pánuco and Lerma, while by the generally used cartographic convention the border between North and Central America is shown as formed by the Isthmus of Tehuantepec.

12 R. Larco Hoyle, *Checan, Studie über erotische Darstellungen in der peruanischen Kunst.* Munich, Geneva, Paris 1965.

13 A. Posnansky, *Die erotischen Keramiken der Mochica und deren Beziehungen zu okzipital deformierten Schädeln* (Festschrift zur Feier des 25jährigen Bestehens der Frankfurter Gesellschaft für Anthropologie und Urgeschichte), pp. 67–74. Frankfort 1925.

14 Hans Feriz, *Zwischen Peru und Mexiko.* Amsterdam 1959.

15 V. W. von Hagen, *The Desert Kingdom of Peru.* Greenwich 1965.

16 Perhaps this exhortation to the new-born son would have begun slightly differently had the Aztecs not thought themselves forced by their political and economic situation to bring up their children in a military spirit. They were the last tribe to migrate into the fertile highlands of Mexico before the Spanish conquest, and their originally small tribe was surrounded by envious enemies. The small and swampy island in the Lake of Texcoco soon proved too narrow for the fast growing number of Aztecs. At first, forming a small minority, they had hired themselves out as mercenaries to the neighbouring rich city-states, which were continually fighting for the fertile lands around the lake. Later, when they themselves had grown sufficiently strong, they subjugated not only their immediate neighbours, but nearly all the tribes of Mexico, making them pay tribute. Owing to this military-political position the Aztec "Eagle and Jaguar Warriors" were greatly esteemed. See also Katz, F., *Die sozialökonomischen Verhältnisse bei den Azteken im 15. und 16. Jahrhundert*, Berlin 1956.

17 Marriages could be dissolved only by a judicial sentence, but requests for divorce were not popular and the judges tried to oppose them.

18 Veytia in *Historia III*, p. 421 ff., provides a list of the laws of Nezahualcoyotl (the Fasting Coyote) recorded by native historians. There are eighteen laws, some with additions. According to Professor J. Kohler, writing in 1892 about the Aztecs' laws, the number mentioned by various historians was 32, going back to Nezahualcoyotl.

19 Anyone who sold the free child of another man as a slave became himself a slave. He and his property were forfeited in favour partly of the child or of its mother, partly in favour of the innocent buyer and of the person who had discovered the fraud, which in this way was to be righted. Orozco y Berra, Manuel, *Historia antigua y de la conquista de México*, 1880 (Libro de Oro, p. 270).

20 Diego de Landa contradicts himself repeatedly in his script, and as other first-hand sources are hardly available, it is difficult to obtain a reliable survey.

21 Gonzalo Fernández de Oviedo y Valdés, *Historia general y natural de las Indias*, ed. by Juan Pérez de Todela Buesco, 5 vols. (vol. 4, book 42), Madrid 1959.

22 *Ibid.* (chap. 11).

23 Sylvanus G. Morley, *The Ancient Maya*, 3rd ed. 1956.

24 Gonzalo Fernández de Oviedo y Valdés, *op. cit.*

25 *Ibid.*

26 *Ibid.* (chap. 12).

27 Chicha was made of the kernels of maize, usually chewed by old people, in particular by old women who had not much to do. The action of the saliva helped to speed up fermentation. Afterwards the softened pulp was spat back into a vessel. In some regions maize beer is made today just as it was two thousand years ago.

28 See Note 2.

29 In his books: *Die Inka von Peru* (Essen 1947), *Der sozialistische Staat der Inka* (Hamburg 1956), and *Daily Life in Peru* (London 1960), Louis Baudin writes about "lice being picked up on hair." The author supposes that this is a misinterpretation or a wrong translation, since pointed steel needles, required for this, were not at hand at that time. In the course of many travels which the author undertook in Peru and Bolivia, he saw how children picked lice out of each other's hair.

30 It must be stressed that this old legend, which is contained in volume I of the *Biblioteca de Cultura peruana*, is, at least in this version, a post-Columbian text, though most probably based on still older narrations.

31 Louis Baudin, *Der sozialistische Staat der Inka.* Hamburg 1956.

32 Among the upper social ranks, at least, gold dust, too, was used besides precious fabrics, jade ornaments as well as feather and gold work. The gold dust was filled in quills and was a trade object. In the *Florentine Codex*, book X, chapter 17, Sahagún gives a detailed description of the merchants trading in these goods.

33 Fra Bernardino de Sahagún, *Codex Florentino*, book X, chap. 26.

34 In his script *La Epoca de los Señorios Independientes* (Mexico D.F. 1967), Alfonso Caso gives the following dates for Acamapichtli: 1376–1396.

35 H. D. Disselhoff, *Geschichte der altamerikanischen Kulturen*, 2nd edition, pp. 76–92, Munich 1967.

36 The floral war was fought between the Aztecs and the Tlaxcaltecs every few years, allegedly so as to present young men, "young flowers" (warriors), to the gods, in fact, however, so as to train their armies.

37 Cieza de León, *Crónica del Perú*, chap. 19, 23, 49.

38 Francisco López de Gómara, *Historia general de las Indias*, chap. 124.

39 Cieza de León, *Crónica del Peru*, part two.

40 Poma de Ayala, *Nueva Corónica y buen Gobierno.*

41 Sacsahuaman, large fortifications near Cuzco.

42 According to the English translation by John H. Rowe, who translated it from the Quechua, retaining the original metre.

43 Several editions exist of this informative epic poem which throws light on the late Maya civilization. Only the best of them should be mentioned here: Schultze-Jena, L., *Popol Vuh, das heilige Buch der Quiché-Indianer von Guatemala*, original text and translation Stuttgart and Berlin 1944.
Popol Vuh. Las Antiguas Histórias de Quiché, translated from the Quiché into Spanish and edited by Adrián Recinos. 4th ed., Mexico and Buenos Aires 1960.
An English translation by Delia Goetz and Sylvanus G. Morley, basing on the Spanish translation by Adrián Recinos, was published by the University of Oklahoma Press in 1950. See also F. Anton, *Altindianische Weisheit und Poesie*, Leipzig and Vienna 1968.

44 Eduard Seler, *Gesammelte Abhandlungen zur amerikanischen Sprach- und Altertumskunde*, vol. IV, edited by Cäcilie Seler-Sachs. Berlin 1923 (2nd edition Akademische Druck- und Verlagsanstalt, Graz 1960), "Mythus und Religion der alten Mexikaner," pp. 3-156.

45 Fray Bernardino de Sahagún, *Codex Florentino*, I and X.

46 See F. Anton, *Alt-Mexiko und seine Kunst*, Leipzig 1965. English translation: *Ancient Mexican Art*, London, New York 1969.

47 One of the most detailed treatises on the gods and religious conceptions of the Maya Indians, to which the author of this book is much indebted, should be mentioned here: Ferdinand Anders, *Das Pantheon der Maya*, Akademische Druck- und Verlagsanstalt, Graz 1963.

48 See F. Anton, *Kunst der Maya*, Leipzig 1968. English translation: *Art of the Maya*, London, New York 1970.

49 From *Reports on the Discovery of Peru*, Hakluyt Society, London 1872. Ed. Sir Clements R. Markham.

SYNOPTICAL TABLE

PERIOD   MESOAMERICA

Mexico,	Guatemala, Honduras, El Salvador,
Northwest – Central region – South –	(Yucatán, Lowlands / Highlands)

Period	Mexico	Guatemala, Honduras, El Salvador
1519 — 45	Spanish Conquest	
1400	Aztecs — Huaxtecs / Totonacs — Tarascans — Mixtecs / Zapotecs	Quiché and Cachiqueles Tazumal (Toltec Influence)
1200	Chichimecs	League of Mayapán Pipiles (Late Bilbao)
900	Chichimecs Toltecs	
600	Colima El Tajín Teotihuacán IV	Post-classical Maya Civilization
400	Monte Albán III Teotihuacán III	Middle Bilbao Uloa Style Copán
200	Michoacán Mixtecs Zapotecs Teotihuacán II Monte Albán II	Classical Maya Civilization Early Bilbao El Baúl Tazumal Monument
0		Olmecs
200	Teotihuacán I Olmecs	
500	Chupicúaro La Venta	Kaminaljuyú
1000	Olmecs Tlatilco	
1500		
3000	Early Cultivators	
5000		
11 000	Man from Tepexpan – Hunters	
25 000	Indian Immigration	Vestiges Acahualinca

 = Spread of a style of art by priest-kings

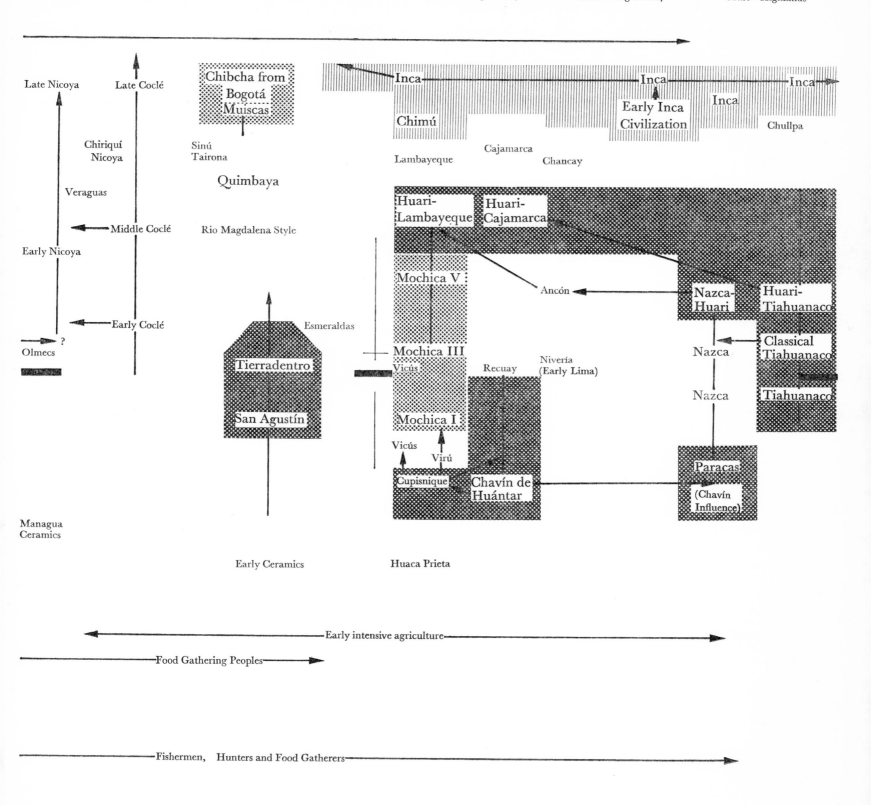

GOLD COUNTRIES

Costa Rica,   Panama,   Colombia,   Ecuador

ANCIENT PERU

North
Coast – Highlands,

Central region
Coast – Highlands,

South
Coast – Highlands

Late Nicoya

Late Coclé

Chibcha from
Bogotá
Muiscas

Inca — Inca — Inca

Chimú

Early Inca
Civilization

Inca

Chullpa

Chiriquí
Nicoya

Sinú
Tairona

Cajamarca

Lambayeque   Chancay

Veraguas

Quimbaya

Huari-
Lambayeque

Huari-
Cajamarca

Middle Coclé

Río Magdalena Style

Early Nicoya

Mochica V

Ancón

Nazca-
Huari

Huari-
Tiahuanaco

Early Coclé

Esmeraldas

Mochica III

Nivería
(Early Lima)

Nazca

Classical
Tiahuanaco

Olmecs

?

Tierradentro

Vicús

Recuay

Nazca

Tiahuanaco

San Agustín

Mochica I

Vicús   Virú

Cupisnique

Chavín de
Huántar

Paracas

(Chavín
Influence)

Managua
Ceramics

Early Ceramics   Huaca Prieta

← Early intensive agriculture →

← Food Gathering Peoples →

← Fishermen,   Hunters and Food Gatherers →

▓▓▓ = Minor kingdoms with secular rulers ||||||||||| = The empire of the Incas and the territories under Aztec rule

CATALOGUE OF
ILLUSTRATIONS

1 Clay Statuette with Two Faces (detail)
Example of so-called "Pretty Lady." Height of detail approx. 5 cm. Tlatilco, highlands of Mexico. Pre-classic period, approx. 1200–500 B.C. Collection Dr. Kurt Stavenhagen, Mexico D.F.

2 Seated Woman
Hard baked clay with remnants of original painting. Height 10.6 cm. Tlatilco, highlands of Mexico. Pre-classic period, approx. 1200–500 B.C. Collection M. Covarrubias, Museo Nacional de Antropología, Mexico D.F.

3 Female Dancer
Solid clay statuette, painted. Height 10 cm. Tlatilco, highlands of Mexico. Pre-classic period, approx. 1200–500 B.C. Private collection, Mexico D.F.

4 Clay Statuette Type "Pretty Lady"
Height 11 cm. Tlatilco, highlands of Mexico. Pre-classic period, approx. 1200–500 B.C. Collection Dr. Kurt Stavenhagen, Mexico D.F.

5 Female Dancers
Solid clay statuette, remnants of reddish, yellow and whiteish painting. Height 16.5 and 15.5 cm. Tlatilco, highlands of Mexico. Pre-classic period, approx. 1200–500 B.C. Private collection, Mexico D.F.

6 Grave with Offerings
Faithful copy of grave at Tlatilco, highlands of Mexico. Pre-classic period 1200–500 B.C. Museo Nacional de Antropología, Mexico D.F.

7 Female Figure with Two Faces
Solid clay statuette. Height 9.5 cm. Tlatilco, highlands of Mexico. Pre-classic period, approx. 1200–500 B.C. Collection Dr. Kurt Stavenhagen, Mexico D.F.

8 Head of a Young Girl
Solid clay statuette, painted. Height 14 cm. Tlatilco, highlands of Mexico. Pre-classic period, approx. 1200–500 B.C. Museo Nacional de Antropología, Mexico D.F.

9 Torso of a Naked Woman
Height approx. 16 cm. Tlatilco, highlands of Mexico. Pre-classic period, approx. 1200–500 B.C. Collection Dr. Kurt Stavenhagen, Mexico D.F.

10 Seated Female Figure
Solid clay statuette. Height 9 cm. Tlatilco, highlands of Mexico. Pre-classic period, approx. 1200–500 B.C. Collection Dr. Kurt Stavenhagen, Mexico D.F.

11 Seated Young Girl
Solid clay statuette. Height 11 cm. Tlatilco, highlands of Mexico. Pre-classic period, approx. 1200–500 B.C. Collection Dr. Kurt Stavenhagen, Mexico D.F.

12 Fragment of a Female Figure
Solid clay statuette. Height 14 cm. Confederate state of Morelos, Mexico. Pre-classic period, approx. 800–400 B.C. Private collection, Mexico D.F.

13 Seated Mother with Child
Clay sculpture with white, chalk-like priming. Height

14 cm. Tlapacoya, highlands of Mexico. Pre-classic period, **approx. 1000–200 B.C.** Private collection, Mexico D.F.

14 *Fragment of a Young Female Figure*
Solid clay with whiteish priming. Height 18 cm. Tlapacoya, highlands of Mexico. Pre-classic period, approx. 2000–1000 B.C. Collection Stolper Galleries, Munich

15 *Front and Back of Standing Female Figure*
Hollow clay figure. Height 35 cm. Chupícuaro, Michoacán. Pre-classic period, approx. 800 B.C.—A.D. 200. Private collection, Los Angeles

16 *Statuette of a Young Girl*
Reddish clay. Height 31 cm. Department Sonsonate, El Salvador. Pre-classic period, approx. 200 B.C.—A.D. 100. Museo Nacional de El Salvador

17 *Small Clay Figure of Naked Woman*
Solid clay with slight vestiges of painting. Height 7.5 cm. Region of Chupícuaro, Michoacán, Mexico. Pre-classic period, approx. 800–200 B.C. Private collection, U.S.A.

18 *Large Figure of a Seated Goddess*
Jadeite stone. Height 55 cm., width 42 cm., weight 60 kg. Las Limas, southern Gulf coast, Mexico. La Venta or so-called "Olmec" civilization, approx. 500 B.C.—A.D. 200. Museo Regional de Jalapa. Veracruz

19 *Head of a Young Female Figure*
Clay. Height 17.5 cm. Central Veracruz. (Ignacio de la Llave?) Tajín civilization of central Gulf coast, approx. A.D. 600–1000. Museo Regional de Jalapa, Veracruz

20 *Rattle Shaped like a Naked, probably Pregnant Woman*
Light coloured clay. Height approx. 10 cm. Highlands of Guatemala. Pre-classic Maya civilization, "Olmec" style, approx. 800–100 B.C. Museo Nacional de Guatemala

21 *Bas-relief from the Altar of La Venta*
Height 107 cm. La Venta on the southern coast of the Gulf of Mexico. La Venta or so-called "Olmec" civilization, approx. 500 B.C.—A.D. 200. Park Museum, Villa Hermosa. Tabasco, Mexico

22 *Seated Couple*
Solid clay statuette, painted red. Height 16.4 and 16.6 cm. Place of discovery unkown, Colima, Mexico. Pre-classic period of the northwest coast. Style of Colima, approx. 200 B.C.—A.D. 400. Private collection, Munich

23 *Woman Seated on the Knees of Another Woman*
Clay, with remnants of red and blackish painting. Height 49 cm. Region of Barrancas, Jalisco, Mexico. Jalisco style of the northwest coast, approx. 200 B.C. to A.D. 1000. Collection Stendahl, Los Angeles

24 *Seated Naked Woman*
Clay with reddish paint. Height 50 cm. Place of discovery unknown, Nayarit, Mexico. Nayarit style of the northwest coast, approx. 200 B.C.–A.D. 1000. Gallery Wels, Salzburg

25 *Noble Lady with Little Dog* (detail)
Remnants of ochre, brownish and grey painting, Height of whole figure 54 cm., of the detail approx. 25 cm. Jomulco, Nayarit, Mexico. Civilization of the northwest coast, Nayarit style, approx. A.D. 400–1000. Gallery Wels, Salzburg

26 *Recumbent, probably Pregnant Woman in the Form of a Vessel*
Clay. Length 25 cm. Place of discovery unknown. Colima, Mexico. Colima style of the northwest coast, approx. A.D. 200–800. Collection Stendahl, Los Angeles

27 *Seated Naked Woman*
Clay with reddish and whiteish painting. Height 28 cm. Place of discovery unknown, Nayarit, Mexico. New style of the northwest coast, not yet exactly defined, approx. 200 B.C.—A.D. 1000. Collection Dr. Kurt Stavenhagen, Mexico D.F.

28 *Seated Woman*
Burnt clay painted red, orange and grey-black. Height 25 cm. Place of discovery unknown, northwest coast of Mexico. So-called "Mongoloid" type, civilization of the northwest coast, approx. A.D. 200—800. Private collection, Munich

29 *Vessel Shaped as a Pregnant Woman*
Blackish-grey clay. Height 20.5 cm. Place of discovery unknown, northwest coast of Mexico. Civilization of the northwest coast, Nayarit style, approx. A.D. 300–1000. Collection Dr. Kurt Stavenhagen, Mexico D.F.

30 *Mother with Child on her Arm, Carrying a Large Pot*
Clay with polychrome painting. Height 35 cm. Colima, Mexico. Civilization of the northwest coast, late Colima style, approx. A.D. 600–1200. Collection Dr. Kurt Stavenhagen, Mexico D.F.

31 *Stylized Seated Female Figure*
Baked clay. Height 17 cm. Jalisco, Mexico. Civilization of the northwest coast, Jalisco style, approx. A.D. 200–1000. Collection Dr. Kurt Stavenhagen, Mexico D.F.

32 *Seated Mother with Child*
Clay with remnants of original priming. Height 14 cm. Border region between Colima and Nayarit, Mexico. Civilization of the northwest coast, Colima style, approx. A.D. 200–1000. Collection Dr. Kurt Stavenhagen, Mexico, D.F.

33 *Seated Mother with Child*
Clay with reddish paint. Height 12 cm. Nayarit, Mexico. Civilization of the northwest coast, Nayarit style, approx. A.D. 200–1000. Collection Dr. Kurt Stavenhagen, Mexico D.F.

34 *Seated Couple with Child*
Height 14 cm. Jalisco, Mexico. Civilization of the northwest coast, Jalisco style, approx. A.D. 200–1000. Collection Dr. Kurt Stavenhagen, Mexico D.F.

35 *Musicians and Female Dancer*
Solid, unpainted clay sculpture. Height 12 cm. Colima, Mexico. Civilization of the northwest coast, Colima

style, approx. A.D. 200–800. Collection Dr. Kurt Stavenhagen, Mexico D.F.

36 *Vessel Shaped as a Resting Young Girl*
Clay with remnants of painting. Height 26 cm. Colima, Mexico. Civilization of the northwest coast, Colima style, approx. A.D. 600–1200. Collection Dr. Kurt Stavenhagen, Mexico D.F.

37 *Seated Young Woman*
Height 12 cm. Colima, Mexico. Civilization of the northwest coast, Colima style, approx. A.D. 200–800. Collection Dr. Kurt Stavenhagen, Mexico D.F.

38 *Two Naked Female Dancers*
Clay with reddish paint. Height 27 cm. Place of discovery unknown, Jalisco, Mexico. Civilization of the northwest coast, Jalisco style, approx. A.D. 200–1000. Collection Dr. Kurt Stavenhagen, Mexico D.F.

39 *Seated Young Girl*
Reddish-brown clay. Height 29 cm. Place of discovery unknown, Colima, Mexico. Civilization of the northwest coast, Colima style, approx. A.D. 600–1200. Collection Dr. Kurt Stavenhagen, Mexico, D. F.

40 *One-storied House*
Stone with vestiges of paint. Height approx. 25 cm. Place of discovery unknown, probably Nayarit. Civilization of the northwest coast, Nayarit style, undated. Collection Dr. Kurt Stavenhagen, Mexico D.F.

41 *Standing Woman*
Height approx. 75 cm. Place of discovery unknown, Nayarit, Mexico. Civilization of the northwest coast, approx. A.D. 800–1200. Collection Dr. Kurt Stavenhagen, Mexico D.F.

42 *Clay Sculpture of Recumbent Pregnant Woman*
Reddish paint. Length 22 cm. Place of discovery unknown, Colima, Mexico. Civilization of the northwest coast, Colima style, approx. A.D. 200–800. Collection Dr. Kurt Stavenhagen, Mexico D.F.

43 *Couple on a Seat*
Height 12 cm. Place of discovery unknown, Colima, Mexico. Civilization of the northwest coast, Colima style, approx. A.D. 200–800. Collection Dr. Kurt Stavenhagen, Mexico D.F.

44 *Kneeling Woman*
Height 30 cm. Place of discovery unknown, Jalisco, Mexico. Civilization of the northwest coast, Jalisco style, approx. A.D. 200–1000. Collection Dr. Kurt Stavenhagen, Mexico D.F.

45 *Seated Couple of Lovers*
Clay painted brownish-red. Height 12 cm. Place of discovery unknown, Colima, Mexico. Pre-classic period of the northwest coast, Colima style, approx. A.D. 200–800. Collection Dr. Kurt Stavenhagen, Mexico D.F.

46 *a) Woman in the so-called Gingerbread Shape*
Clay painted with ochre. Height 17 cm. Place of discovery unknown, Jalisco, Mexico. Early civilization of the northwest coast, approx. 200 B.C.–A.D. 400. Private collection, Munich

46 *b, 46c, 47a, 47b) Four Couples of Solid Clay*
Height approx. 9–15 cm. Place of discovery unknown, Colima, Nayarit, Jalisco, Mexico. Civilization of the northwest coast, approx. A.D. 200–800. Collection Dr. Kurt Stavenhagen, Mexico D.F.

48 *Seated Woman with Child*
Dark green stone with vermillion painting. Height 41 cm., width 12 cm. Acapulco, Orilla del Rio de San Pedro, Guerrero, Mexico. Staatliche Museen Preussischer Kulturbesitz, Museum für Völkerkunde, West Berlin

49 *Singing or Dancing Woman*
Light-coloured clay, not painted. Height approx. 80 cm. Place of discovery unknown, central coast of Gulf of Mexico. Tajín civilization, approx. A.D. 700–1200. Collection Dr. Kurt Stavenhagen, Mexico D.F.

50 *Recumbent Figure of a Young Girl*
Yellowish-brown stone. Height 16.5 cm., length 42 cm. Place of discovery unknown, central Veracruz, Mexico. Tajín civilization (Olmec influence), approx. 100 B.C. to A.D. 400. Cleveland Museum of Art, Cleveland

51 *Mother with Child*
Light-coloured clay with black bituminous painting. Height 24.5 cm. Region of Las Remojadas, central coast of Gulf of Mexico. Tajín civilization, Remojadas style, approx. A.D. 200–600. Southwest Museum, Los Angeles

52 *Female Dancer or Goddess*
Height approx. 30 cm. Place of discovery unknown, central coast of Gulf of Mexico. Tajín civilization, approx. A.D. 800–1200. Collection Dr. Kurt Stavenhagen, Mexico D.F.

53 *Standing Female Dancer, with Bells on her Ankles*
Light-grey clay, with bituminous painting. Height 42 cm. Central coast of Gulf of Mexico, Tajín civilization, approx. A.D. 600–800. Museo Regional de Jalapa, Veracruz

54 *Fragment of a Head, Type of "Caras Sonrientes"*
Ochre-coloured clay, no painting. Height 11.5 cm. La Hoja, Veracruz, Mexico. Tajín civilization of central coast of the Gulf of Mexico, approx. A.D. 800–1200. Private collection, Munich

55 *a) Figure of a Richly Dressed Female Dignitary*
Almost whiteish clay. Height 31.5 cm. Burial place Secundario 6 del Vertedero de Nopiloa. Tierra Blanca region, Veracruz. Tajín civilization of the central Gulf coast, approx. A.D. 800–1200. Museo Regional de Jalapa, Veracruz

55 *b) Doll with Moveable Limbs Shaped as Standing Woman*
Almost whiteish clay with remnants of original painting. Height 25 cm. Burial place Secundario 6 del Vertedero de Nopiloa. Region of Tierra Blanca, Veracruz. Tajín civilization of the central coast of the Gulf of Mexico, approx. A.D. 800–1200. Museo Regional de Jalapa, Veracruz

56 Seated Female Figure
Ceramic with polychrome painting. Height 19.5 cm. Tenenexpan, Veracruz. Civilization of the northern coast of the Gulf, Huaxtec (Pánuco V), post-classic period, A.D. 100–1250. Museo Regional de Jalapa, Veracruz

57 Two Necklaces of Gold Beads, Pieces of Turquoise and of Shells and a Bracelet of Embossed Gold Plate
Grave No. 7 of Monte Albán, Oaxaca. Post-classic period, Mixtec civilization, approx. A.D. 1200–1450
Bracelet: Collection Dr. Kurt Stavenhagen, Mexico D.F. Necklaces: Museo Regional de Oaxaca, Mexico

58 Fragment of so-called Grave-Urn
Light-grey hard baked clay. Height 22 cm. Oaxaca, Mexico. Zapotec civilization, approx. A.D. 600–1200. Museum für Völkerkunde, Vienna

59 Detail from the Codex Bodley 2858
Painted deerskin. Size of page 29×26 cm. Oaxaca, Mexico. Mixtec civilization, approx. A.D. 1500. Bodleian Library, University of Oxford

60 Young Deity
Light-grey clay with remnants of original painting. Height 91 cm., width 32 cm. Central Gulf coast. Tajín civilization, approx. A.D. 600–1000. Collection Dr. Peter Ludwig, Rautenstrauch-Joest Museum, Cologne

61 Mother with Child
Clay fragment. Height 6 cm. Teotihuacán, highlands of Mexico. Teotihuacán civilization, approx. A.D. 200 to 600. Collection Dr. Kurt Stavenhagen, Mexico D.F.

62 Sun Pyramid of Teotihuacán
Height 65 m. Teotihuacán civilization, approx. 100 B.C. to A.D. 600.

63 The Water Goddess Chalchiuhtlicue, the "Lady with the Skirt of Jade"
Cut in chalcedony, a kind of alabaster. Height 27.5 cm. Probably from the highlands of Mexico. Teotihuacán civilization, approx. A.D. 400–600. Collection Bilimek, Museum für Völkerkunde, Vienna

64 Humpbacked Old Woman
Stone sculpture. Height 36 cm. Post-classic period of Mexico. Museum für Völkerkunde, Leipzig

65 Mictlanciuatl
Volcanic stone. Height 32 cm. Highlands of Mexico. Aztec civilization, approx. A.D. 1350–1521. Museo Nacional de Antropología, Mexico D.F.

66 Statue of Coatlicue
Grey stone (andesite). Height 2.52 m. Tenochtitlán (Mexico D.F.). Aztec civilization, approx. A.D. 1450 to 1519. Museo Nacional de Antropología, Mexico D.F.

67 Head of the Moon Goddess Coyolxauhqui
Porphyritic basalt. Size 78×39 cm. Tenochtitlán (Mexico City). Aztec civilization, A.D. 1370–1521. Museo Nacional de Antropología, Mexico D.F.

68 Pendant
Fragment of sea-shell, incised and polished. Height 10 cm. Region of the modern town of Veracruz, Mexico.

Huaxtec civilization (Pánuco V), approx. A.D. 1000 to 1250. Middle American Research Institute, Tulane University, New Orleans

69 Stone Figure of the Goddess Tlazoltéotl, Giving Birth to a Child
Green speckled aplite. Height 21 cm. Place of discovery unknown. Aztec civilization, approx. A.D. 1450–1521. Collection Robert Woods Eliss, Dumbarton Oaks, Washington D.C.

70 Fragment of the Head of the Maize Goddess Chicomecóatl
Rough clay. Height 16 cm. Place of discovery unknown, probably region of Oaxaca. Zapotec civilization, approx. A.D. 800–1400. Collection Dr. Kurt Stavenhagen, Mexico D.F.

71 Statue of the Goddess Coatlicue
Block of basalt. Height 117 cm. Cozcatlán, Puebla, Mexico. Aztec civilization, approx. A.D. 1450–1521. Museo Nacional de Antropología, Mexico D.F.

72 a) Beaker Representing Dancers or Couples of Lovers
Clay with polychrome painting. Height 18.5 cm. Lake of Yoyoa, Santa Barbara, Honduras. Classic Maya civilization, approx. A.D. 500–800. Middle American Research Institute, New Orleans

72 b) Cup
Clay with polychrome painting. Height 7.3 cm. "El Tronconal," Dep. Ahuachapán, El Salvador. Probably influenced by the classic Maya civilization, approx. A.D. 600–900. Museo Nacional de El Salvador

73 Female Figures Represented on Plate 18 of the Dresden Maya Manuscript
Sächsische Landesbibliothek, Dresden

74 Head of a Young Girl
Fragment of clay. Height 13.5 cm. Highlands of Chiapas, Mexico. Late classic Maya civilization, approx. A.D. 800–1100. Museo Regional de Chiapas, Tuxtla Gutierrez

75 Standing Figure of a Young Girl
Solid clay. Height 18 cm. El Salvador, pre-classic period, approx. 800–200 B.C. Museo Nacional de Antropología, San Salvador

76 The Goddess Ixchel
Represented on Plate 30 of the Codex Tro-Cortesianus. Vegetable fibre covered with a layer of clay, polychrome painting. Size of detail 12×11.5 cm. Probably Yucatán, Mexico. Museo de América, Madrid

77 The Deity Itzamná
Wall painting. Height of the figure 80 cm. Post-classic Maya civilization, approx. A.D. 1200–1400. Tulum, Quintana Roo, Mexico

78 Vessel Shaped as a Woman Resting, Carrying a Jug on her Shoulder
Reddish clay with remnants of black and green painting. Height 12.5 cm. Cobán, Alta Verapaz, highlands of Guatemala. Late classic Maya civilization, approx. A.D. 800–1000. Staatliche Museen Preussischer Kulturbesitz, Museum für Völkerkunde, West Berlin

79 Vessel Shaped as a Seated Woman
Clay burnt blackish and polished. Height 24 cm. Most

probably highlands of Guatemala. Probably late classic Maya civilization, approx. A.D. 900–1100. University Museum, Philadelphia

80 *Noblewoman with Necklace, Earplugs and Nose Ornament*
Jade. Height 10 cm. Northern highlands of Guatemala. Classic Maya civilization, approx. A.D. 300–900. The University Museum, Philadelphia

81 *Detail of Stele H*
Height 2.60 m. Copán, Honduras. Classic Maya civilization, A.D. 782

82 *Rattle*
Clay with remnants of whiteish painting. Height 16 cm. Island of Jaina, Campeche, Mexico. Late classic Maya civilization, approx. A.D. 800–1000. Collection Stendahl, Los Angeles

83 *Seated Woman*
Solid clay figure. Height 12 cm. Island of Jaina, Campeche, Mexico. Late classic Maya civilization, approx. A.D. 700–900. Collection Dr. Kurt Stavenhagen, Mexico D.F.

84 *Ocarina Shaped as a Richly Clothed Lady*
Clay with remnants of blue and reddish colour. Height 17 cm. Place of discovery unknown. Style of the Island of Jaina, Campeche, Mexico. Late classic Maya civilization, approx. A.D. 800–1000. Collection Dr. Kurt Stavenhagen, Mexico D.F.

85 *Ocarina Shaped as a Deity in Festive Attire*
Height 22 cm. Island of Jaina, Campeche, Mexico. Late classic Maya civilization, approx. A.D. 800–1000. Museo Nacional de Antropología, Mexico D.F.

86 *Noble Lady with Dwarf*
Clay with remnants of original painting. Height approx. 20 cm. Island of Jaina, Campeche, Mexico. Late classic Maya civilization, approx. A.D. 800–1000. Collection Dr. Kurt Stavenhagen, Mexico D.F.

87 *Sumptuously Clothed Lady*
Painted clay. In the form of an ocarina. Height 20 cm. Island of Jaina, Campeche, Mexico. Late classic Maya civilization, approx. A.D. 800–1000. Private collection, Los Angeles

88 a) *Ocarina Shaped as a Lewd Old Man and a Young Girl*
Terracotta. Height 9.5 cm. Place of discovery unknown. Style of Island of Jaina, Campeche, Mexico. Late classic Maya civilization, approx. A.D. 800–1000. Collection Dr. Kurt Stavenhagen, Mexico D.F.

88 b) *Courting Couple*
Solid clay. Height 18 cm. Island of Jaina, Campeche, Mexico. Late classic Maya civilization, approx. A.D. 800–1000. Collection Dr. Kurt Stavenhagen, Mexico D.F.

89 a) *Ocarina Shaped as a Noble Lady Accompanied by a "Coyote"*
Height 14 cm. Place of discovery unknown. Style of the Island of Jaina, Campeche, Mexico. Late Maya civilization, approx. A.D. 800–1000. Collection Dr. Kurt Stavenhagen, Mexico D.F.

89 b) *Noble Lady*
Clay with vestiges of earlier painting. Height 19.5 cm. Island of Jaina, Campeche, Mexico. Late classic Maya civilization, approx. A.D. 800–1000. Collection Dr. Kurt Stavenhagen, Mexico D.F.

89 c) *Mother with Children Preparing Tortillas (Maize Cakes)*
Solid clay. Height 16.5 cm. Place of discovery unknown. Style of Island of Jaina, Campeche, Mexico. Late classic Maya civilization, approx. A.D. 800–1000. Collection Dr. Kurt Stavenhagen, Mexico D.F.

90 *Richly Clothed Lady*
Height 18 cm. Island of Jaina, Campeche, Mexico. Late classic Maya civilization, approx. A.D. 800–1000. Collection Dr. Kurt Stavenhagen, Mexico D.F.

91 *Lady with a Cape-like Wrap*
To be used as an ocarina. Clay with remnants of earlier painting. Height approx. 17 cm. Island of Jaina, Campeche, Mexico. Late classic Maya civilization, approx. A.D. 800–1000. Collection Dr. Kurt Stavenhagen, Mexico D.F.

92 *Small Clay Figure of Standing Woman*
Height approx. 16 cm. Lake of Valencia, Venezuela. Approx. A.D. 500–1200. Museo Nacional, Caracas

93 *Naked Woman, Seated*
Clay painted red. Height 16.5 cm. Place of discovery unknown. Nicaragua. No dates. Private collection, Munich

94 *Mother Carrying her Child in her Arms*
Polychrome painted clay figure. Height 13 cm. Tierras Blancas, province of Cartago, Costa Rica. Approx. A.D. 800–1400. Übersee Museum, Bremen

95 *Two Seated Women*
Polychrome painted clay. Size 12.5×15 cm. Filadelfia, Guanacaste, Costa Rica. Approx. A.D. 800–1400. Collection Stendahl, Los Angeles

96 *Vessel Shaped as a Seated Woman*
Solid clay figure, remnants of simple painting. Height 26 cm. Place of discovery unknown. Cauca Valley, Colombia. Chibcha civilization, approx. A.D. 1200–1500. Instituto Colombiano de Antropología, Bogotá

97 *Female Deity with Teeth of Beast of Prey*
Bas-relief on a large stele. Reddish stone. Height approx. 1.80 m. San Agustín, Colombia. Approx. 200 B.C.–A.D. 600. San Agustín

98 *Front and Back of a Standing Female Figure*
Volcanic stone. Height 34 cm. Atlantic slope or possibly highlands of Costa Rica. Unknown civilization, approx. A.D. 1000–1500. Museum für Völkerkunde, Vienna

99 *Standing Female Figure*
Volcanic stone. Height 50 cm. Guapiles, Costa Rica. Unknown civilization, approx. A.D. 1000–1500. Collection Stendahl, Los Angeles

100 a) *So-called Ceremonial Knife*
Height 9 cm. Tolima, upper course of Magdalena River, Colombia. Tolima style, approx. A.D. 1000–1500. Private collection, Bogotá

100 b) *Gold Amulet*
Height approx. 7.3 cm. Coclé region, Panama. Coclé civilization, approx. A.D. 1000–1500. Textile Museum, Washington

101 a) *Sewing Needles*
Length 12–20 cm. Central coast of Peru. Approx. A.D. 1200–1400. Collection Bob Gesinus, Amsterdam

101 b) *Sewing Box*
Wood. Length approx. 18 cm. Northern coast of Peru. Probably Chimu civilization, approx. A.D. 1200–1460. Collection C.D.O.

102 *Large Vessel of Clay*
Height 30.5 cm. Northern highlands of Peru. Recuay style, approx. A.D. 300–800. Lindenmuseum, Stuttgart

103 *Vessel Representing a Family in their Home*
Clay, burned black and polished. Height 26 cm. Northern coast of Peru. Chimu civilization, approx. A.D. 1200 to 1460. Private collection, Switzerland

104 *Seated Couple of Lovers*
Bulbous vessel of clay with spout and handle. Height 19 cm. Northern coast of Peru. Civilization of Moche, approx. A.D. 200–800. Textile Museum, Washington D.C.

105 *Woman Carrying a Heavy Burden*
Bulbous clay vessel. Height 14 cm. Trujillo, northern coast of Peru. Civilization of Moche, approx. A.D. 200 to 800. British Museum, London

106 *Priest, Prisoner and Woman in a Mountain Landscape*
Vessel of clay with reddish and yellowish painting. Height 30 cm. Northern coast of Peru. Civilization of Moche, approx. A.D. 200–800. Museum of the American Indian, New York

107 *Jaguar Raping a Naked Woman*
Upper part either of a digger's spade or of a sword of balsa wood. Wood inlaid with mother of pearl. Height 18 cm. Northern coast of Peru. Civilization of Moche, approx. A.D. 200–800. Textile Museum, Washington D.C.

108 *Doll*
Raw cotton, woollen threads and woven tapestry. Length 28 cm. Northern coast of Peru. Chimu civilization, approx. A.D. 1200–1460. Museum für Völkerkunde, Vienna

109 *Fragment of Embroidered Cotton Fabric*
Part of a shroud. Size of this fragment 18 × 15 cm. Peninsula of Paracas, southern coast of Peru. Civilization of the Paracas necropolis, approx. 200 B.C.–A.D. 200. Collection of Mr. and Mrs. Jerome Pustilnik, New York

110 a) *Seated Woman*
Vessel with tube serving as spout, polychrome painting in various red tones, eggshell-white, blueish-grey and violet. Height 16 cm. Southern coast of Peru. Civilization of Nazca, approx. A.D. 100–500. Collection C.D.O.

110 b) *Fragment of a Vessel with Handle, Showing an Erotic Scene*
Height 14 cm. Northern coast of Peru. Early phase of civilization of Moche, approx. A.D. 200–400. Milwaukee Public Museum

111 *Vessel with Handle Representing a Couple*
Ochre and reddish clay. Height 19 cm. Northern coast of Peru. Civilization of Moche, approx. A.D. 200–800. Lindenmuseum, Stuttgart

112 *Mummy of a Noble Female*
Height with basket approx. 120 cm. Peninsula of Paracas, southern coast of Peru. Paracas necropolis civilization, approx. 200 B.C.–A.D. 200. Museo de América, Madrid

Sources of Illustrations

Museum für Völkerkunde, Leipzig: 64, 73
Verlag Georg D. W. Callwey, Munich: 112
All the other photographs: the author.

BIBLIOGRAPHY

1 Acosta, José de, *Historia natural y moral de las Indias*, Mexico and Buenos Aires, 1960

2 Alva Ixtlilxóchitl. See Ixtlilcóchitl

3 Alvarado Tezozomoc, Fernando. See Tezozomoc

4 Ayala, Poma de, Felipe Guzmán. See Poma de Ayala

5 *Anales de los Xahil* (Anales de los Cakchikeles), Trad. de Raynaud, Asturias, Miguel, Angel y Gonzáles de Mendoza, Mexico, 1946. English translation by Delia Goetz, Norman (Oklahoma), 1953

6 Betánzos, Juan de, *Suma y Narración de los Incas*. Edited by Marcos Jiménez de la Espada, Madrid, 1880. (Biblioteca Hispano-Ultramarina II, vol. V)

7 Casas, Bartolomé de las, *Historia de las Indias*, Mexico and Buenos Aires, 1951

8 Chilam Balam, *El libro de los libros*. Translated and edited by Alfredo Barrera Vásquez and Silvia Rendón, Fondo de Cultura Económica, Mexico and Buenos Aires, 1948

9 Cieza de León, Pedro de, *La Crónica del Perú*, Mexico D.F., 1932. *Segunda parte de la crónica del Perú, que trata del Señorio de los Incas* ... Ed. by Marcos Jiménez de la Espada (Biblioteca Hispano-Ultramarina, vol. V), Madrid, 1880

10 Cobo, Bernabé, *Historia del Nuevo Mundo*, 4 vols., Sociedad de Bibliófilos Andaluces, Sevilla, 1890–95

11/12 *Codices Becker I/II* (Facsimile edition with detailed commentary by Karl A. Nowotny), Graz, 1961; cf. also Nowotny, Karl A., *Der Codex Becker I* (Le Manuscrit du Cacique). In: *Archiv für Völkerkunde, XIII (1958)*, pp. 222 ff.; Nowotny, Karl A., *Der Codex Becker II*. In: *Archiv für Völkerkunde, XII (1957)*, pp. 172 ff.

13 *Codex Bodley 2858*, ed. and elucidated by Alfonso Caso, Mexico, 1960

14 *Códice Chimalpopoca. Anales de Cuauhtitlan y Leyenda de los Soles*. Spanish translation from the Nahuatl by Primo Feliciano Velázquez, Mexico D.F., 1945

15 *Codex Dresdensis. Die Maya-Handschrift der Sächsischen Landesbibliothek Dresden*. Complete edition, ed. by H. Deckert, Berlin, 1962. Selected edition of 24 plates, ed. by R. Krusche, Leipzig, 1966

16 *Codex Tro-Cortesianus* (Codex Madrid), Introduction by F. Anders, Akadem. Druck- und Verlagsanstalt, Graz, 1967

17 *Codex Vindobonensis Mexicanus I*, Akadem. Druck- und Verlagsanstalt, Graz, 1963

18 Colón, Cristóbal, *Diario de Colón*, *Libro de la primera navigación y descubrimiento de las Indias*, 2 vols., one of which in facsimile, ed. by Carlos Sanz, Madrid, 1962
La carta de Don Cristóbal Colón anunciando el descubrimiento del Nuevo Mundo.
Reproduction of the edition Barcelona, 1493, Madrid, 1956

19 Cortés, Hernán, *Cartas de Relación de la Conquista de la Nueva España (1519–1527)*. Compl. facsimile edition of the "Codex Vindobonensis S. N. 1600," Akademische

Druck- und Verlagsanstalt, Graz, 1960. Numerous other editions, most of them abbreviated.

20 Díaz del Castillo, Bernal, *Historia Verdadera de la Conquista de la Nueva España*, Mexico D.F., 1950.

21 Durán, Diego, *Historia de las Indias de Nueva España e Islas de Tierra Firme*, Mexico D.F., 1951

22 Gomara, Francisco López de, *Historia general de las Indias*, 2 vols., Barcelona, 1954

23 Historia Tolteca-Chichimeca. *Anales de Cuauhtinchan*. Ed. by H. Berlin and S. Rendón, Mexico D.F., 1947

24 Ixtlilxóchitl, Fernando de Alva, *Obras Históricas*. Ed. by Alfredo Chavero, 2 vols., Mexico D.F., 1891–92

25 Landa, Diego de, *Relación de las cosas de Yucatán*. Various editions. (English translation provided with many notes, by A. M. Tozzer, Cambridge Mass., 1941.)

26 Martyr, Petrus de Angleria, *Opera*. Reprint of "Legatio Babylonica," ed. Alcalá 1516 and other works, Akademische Druck- und Verlagsanstalt, Graz, 1966

27 Motolinía, Toribio de Benavente, *Historia de los Indios de la Nueva España*, ed. by Daniel Sánchez García, Barcelona, 1914

28 Navarrete, Martín Fernández de, *Colección de los Viajes y Descubrimientos que hicieron por mar los Españoles desde fines del siglo XV*, 5 vols., Madrid, 1837–1880

29 Oviedo, Gonzalo—Hernández de Oviedo y Valdés, *Historia general y natural de las Indias, Islas y Tierra Firme del Mar Océaneo*. Madrid 1851–1855

30 Pizarro, Pedro, *Relación del descubrimiento y conquista de los reinos del Perú* (Arequipa, 1571), Buenos Aires, 1944

31 Poma de Ayala, Felipe Guzmán, *Nueva Corónica y buen Gobierno* (codex péruvien illustré), Paris, 1936

32 *Popol Vuh* (various editions). *Popol Vuh, Las Antiguas Histórias del Quiché* (Ed. by A. Recinos, Mexico, 1947). *Popol Vuh, das heilige Buch der Quiché-Indianer von Guatemala*. Translated and edited by L. Schultze-Jena, Stuttgart and Berlin, 1944

33 Rabinal, Der Mann von, *Ein Tanzspiel der Quiché-Maya: Teatro indígena prehispánico*, Mexico D.F., 1955. With Introduction by Palm, E. W., Frankfort, 1961

34 Sahagún, Bernardino de, *Historia General de las Cosas de la Nueva España*, 2 vols., Mexico, 1964. *Florentine Codex: General History of the Things of New Spain*, translated by A. J. O. Anderson and C. E. Dibble. 12 vols., Salt Lake City, Utah, 1950–1963

35 Tezozomoc, Fernando Alvarado, *Crónica Mexicana*, Mexico, 1878

36 Torquemada, Juan de, *Monarquía Indiana*, 3 vols., Mexico D.F., 1943–44

37 Zárate, Agustín de, *Historia del Descubrimiento y Conquista de la Provincia del Perú*, Mexico, no date given

38 Zurita, Alonso de, *Breve Relación de los Señores de la Nueva España*, Mexico D.F., 1941

Mexican civilizations and miscellania on high civilizations (recent authors)

39 *Alt-Aztekische Gesänge, nach einer in der Biblioteca Nacional aufbewahrten Handschrift übersetzt und erläutert von Leonhard Schultze-Jena*. After his death edited by Gerd Kutscher. Sources concerning the ancient history of America. Stuttgart, 1957

40 Anton, Ferdinand and F. J. Dockstader, *Das Alte Amerika*, Baden-Baden, 1967. English edition: New York, 1968

41 Bernal, Ignacio, *Mexico Before Cortez. Art, History and Legend*, Garden City, N. Y., 1963

42 Bernal, Ignacio and others, *The Mexican National Museum of Anthropology*, London, 1968

43 Burland, Cottie A., *The Gods of Mexico*, London, 1967

44 Bushnell, G. H. S., *Ancient Arts of the Americas*, London, 1965

45 Caso, Alfonso, *El pueblo del sol*, Mexico, 1953. English translation: *People of the Sun*, Norman, Oklahoma, 1957

46 Covarrubias, Miguel, *Indian Art of Mexico and Central America*, New York, 1957; *Mexico South*, New York, 1947

47 Disselhoff, H. D., *Geschichte der altamerikanischen Kulturen*, 2nd ed., Munich, 1967

48 Dockstader, F., *Indian Art in Middle America*, Greenwich, Conn. New York Graphic Society, 56 pp. and 248 plates. USA 1964

49 Drucker, Philip, *La Venta, Tabasco. A study of Olmec ceramics and art*. In collaboration with Robert F. Heizer and Robert J. Squier. Washington 1952

50 Enciso, Jorge, *Design Motifs of Ancient Mexico*, Mexico D.F., 1947, New York, 1953

51 *Esplendor de México Antiguo*, 2 vols., compiled by Carmen Cook de Leonard, Mexico D.F., 1959

52 Katz, Friedrich, *Die sozialökonomischen Verhältnisse bei den Azteken im 15. und 16. Jahrhundert*, Berlin, 1956

53 Katz, Friedrich, *Vorkolumbische Kulturen*, Munich, 1969

54 Kohler, J., *Das Recht der Azteken*, Stuttgart, 1892

55 Krickeberg, Walter, *Märchen der Azteken und Inka-Peruaner, Maya und Muisca*, Jena, 1928

56 Krickeberg, Walter, Hermann Trimborn and others, *Die Religion des alten Amerika*. Ed. by Christel Matthias Schröder, Stuttgart, 1961

57 Kutscher, Gerdt, *Präkolumbische Kunst aus Mexiko und Mittelamerika*, Cat. of Exh., Munich, 1958

58 León-Portilla, Miguel, *Aztec Thought and Culture*, Norman, University of Oklahoma Press, 1963

59 León-Portilla, Miguel, *Rückkehr der Götter*, Cologne and Opladen, 1962, Leipzig, 1964

60 Linné, Sigvald and H.D. Disselhoff, *Alt-Amerika*, Baden-Baden, 1960 (Kunst der Welt)

61 Lothrop, S. K., *Das vorkolumbianische Amerika*, Geneva, 1964

62 Nicholson, Irene, *Firefly in the Night. A Study of Ancient Mexican Poetry and Symbolism*, London, 1959

63 Nowotny, Karl A., *Erläuterungen zum Codex Vindobonensis*

(Vorderseite) and *Die Bilderfolge des Codex Vindobonensis und verwandter Handschriften*. In: *Archiv für Völkerkunde, XIII and XIV*, Vienna, 1958 and 1959

64 Nowotny, Karl A., *Tlacuilolli, die mexikanischen Bilderschriften, Stil und Inhalt*, Berlin, 1961

65 Peterson, F. A., *Ancient Mexico*, New York and London, 1959

66 Piña Chan, Román, *Las Culturas preclásicas de la Cuenca de México*, Mexico D.F., 1955

67 Schlenther, Ursula, *Über die Auflösung der Theokratien im präkolumbischen Amerika*. Ethnographisch-Archäologische Zeitschrift, Berlin 1961

68 Séjourné, Laurette, *Pensamiento y Religión en el México Antiguo*, Mexico and Buenos Aires, 1957

69 Seler, Eduard, *Gesammelte Abhandlungen zur amerikanischen Sprach- und Altertumskunde*, vol. I–V, Berlin, 1902 to 1923. New edition, Graz, 1960–1962

70 Seler-Sachs, Caecilie, *Frauenleben im Reiche der Azteken*, Berlin, 1919

71 Soustelle, Jacques, *La vie quotidienne des Aztèques à la veille de la conquête espagnole*, Paris, 1955. English translation: *The Daily Life of the Aztecs*, London, 1961

72 Trimborn, Hermann, *Das Alte Amerika* (Große Kulturen der Frühzeit), Stuttgart, 1959. See also Krickeberg, Walter

73 Vaillant, George C., *Aztecs of Mexico*, Garden City, N.Y., 1944

74 Wauchope, Robert, *Implications of Radiocarbon Dates from Middle and South America*. Middle America Research Institute, Tulane University, New Orleans, 1954

75 Westheim, Paul, *Ideas fundamentales del arte prehispánico en México*, Mexico D.F., 1957

76 Westheim, Paul, *The Sculpture of Ancient Mexico*, New York, 1963

Maya civilization

77 Anders, F., *Das Pantheon der Maya*, Graz, 1963

78 Anton, Ferdinand, *Kunst der Maya*, Leipzig, 1968. English translation: *Art of the Maya*, London, New York, 1970

79 Barthel, Th. S., *Die gegenwärtige Situation in der Erforschung der Maya-Schrift*. In: *Proceedings of the 32nd International Congress of Americanists* (1956), pp. 476–484, Copenhagen, 1958

80 Brainerd, G.W., *The Maya civilization*, Los Angeles, 1954

81 Chinchilla, C. S., *Aproximación al Arte Maya*, Guatemala, 1964

82 Cordan, W., *Götter und Göttertiere der Maya. Resultate des Mérida-Systems*, Berne and Munich, 1963

83 Deckert, H., *Maya-Handschrift der Sächsischen Landesbibliothek Dresden*. Codex Dresdensis, Geschichte und Bibliographie, Berlin, 1962

84 Dieseldorff, E. P., *Kunst und Religion der Maya-Völker im alten und heutigen Mittelamerika*, 3 vols., Berlin, 1926–1933

85 Duby, G., *Chiapas indígena*, Mexico, 1961

86 Girard, R., *Los Chortis ante el problema Maya*, 5 vols., Mexico D.F., 1949

87 Gordon, G. B. and A. J. Mason, *Examples of Maya Pottery* (The Maya Pottery Collection in the University Museum of Philadelphia), Philadelphia, 1925–1943

88 Haberland, W., *Die regionale Verteilung von Schmuckelementen im Bereich der klassischen Maya-Kulturen*, Hamburg, 1953

89 Kimball, Irmgard Groth, *Maya Terrakotten*, Tübingen, 1960

90 Mengin, E., *Die wichtigsten Ergebnisse und Aufgaben der Maya-Sprachforschung*. In: *Akten des 34. Internationalen Amerikanisten-Kongresses* (1960), pp. 743–762, Vienna, 1962

91 Morley, S. G., *The ancient Maya*, 3rd rev. ed., Stanford, 1956

92 Pollock, H. E. D., R. L. Roys and others, *Mayapan, Yucatán, México*. Carnegie Institution, publication No. 619, Washington, 1962

93 Ruz, L., *La Civilización de los antiguos Mayas*, Mexico D.F., 1963

94 Schlenther, U., *Die geistige Welt der Maya. Einführung in die Schriftzeugnisse einer indianischen Priesterkultur*, Berlin, 1965

95 Schultze-Jena, L., *Indiana I. Leben, Glaube und Sprache der Quiché von Guatemala*, Jena, 1933

96 Soustelle, J. and I. Bernal, *Mexico. Präkolumbische Wandmalereien*. Unesco collection of the World Art, 1958

97 Thompson, E. J. S., *A correlation of the Mayan and European Calendars*, Chicago, 1927

98 Thompson, E. J. S., *The Civilization of the Mayas*, Chicago, 1927, and other editions, e.g. 1958

99 Thompson, E. J. S., *The Rise and Fall of Maya Civilization*, Norman, Okla., 1956, London, 1956.

100 Tozzer, A. M. (publication in honour of A. M. Tozzer), *The Maya and their neighbours*, New York, London, 1940, and Salt Lake City, 1960

101 Wadepuhl, W., *Die alten Maya und ihre Kultur*, Leipzig, 1964

102 Willey, G. R., "The Structure of Ancient Maya Society: Evidence from the Southern Lowlands," in: *American Anthropologist*, n.s., vol. 58, pp. 777–782, Menasha, Wis., 1956

The gold countries (from Nicaragua to Colombia)

103 Acuña, Luis Alberto, *El arte de los indios colombianos*, Mexico D.F., 1942

104 Bennett, Wendell C., *Archeological Regions of Colombia. A Ceramic Survey*. Yale University Publications in Anthropology, No. 30, New Haven, Conn. and London, 1944

105 Gómez, Duque, Luis, *Colombia. Monumentos históricos y arqueológicos*, 2 vols., Mexico D.F., 1955

106 Feriz, Hans, *Zwischen Peru und Mexico*, Amsterdam, 1959

107 Nachtigall, Horst, *Die amerikanischen Megalithkulturen*, Berlin, 1958

108 Nachtigall, Horst, *Alt-Kolumbien. Vorgeschichtliche Indianer-kulturen*, Berlin, 1961

109 Nachtigall, Horst, *Indianerkunst der Nord-Anden*, Berlin, 1961

110 Pérez de Barradas, José, *Orfebreria Prehispánica de Colombia. Estilo Calima*, 2 vols., Madrid, 1954

111 Stone, Doris, *Introduction to the Archaeology of Costa Rica*, San José, 1958

112 Trimborn, Hermann, *Vergessene Königreiche. Studien zur Völkerkunde und Altertumskunde Nordwest-Kolumbiens*, Brunswick, 1948

Peru

113 Anton, Ferdinand, *Alt-Peru und seine Kunst*, Leipzig, 1962, 2nd rev. ed., Leipzig, 1972. English translation: *The Art of Ancient Peru*, London, New York, 1972

114 Baudin, Louis, *Der sozialistische Staat der Inka*, Hamburg, 1957. *So lebten die Inkas . . .*, Stuttgart, 1957

115 Baudin, Louis, *Daily Life in Peru*, London, 1960

116 Baudin, Louis, *Les Incas*, Paris, 1964

117 Bennett, Wendell C. and Junius A. Bird, *Andean Culture History*, New York, 1948 and other editions

118 Bird, J. and L. Bellinger, *Paracas Fabrics and Nazca Needlework. Peruvian Textiles*, Washington, 1954

119 Bushnell, G. H. S., *Peru*, London, 1956 and other editions

120 Disselhoff, H. D., *Alltag im alten Peru*, Munich, 1966

121 Dräger, L., *Das alte Peru. Aus dem Museum für Völkerkunde Leipzig*, Leipzig, 1964

122 Engel, Fr., *Early Sites on the Peruvian Coast*. In: *Southwestern Journal of Anthropology*, vol. 13, pp. 54–58, Albuquerque, New Mexico, 1957

123 Engel, Fr., *Early Sites in the Pisco Valley of Peru — Tambo Colorado*. In: *American Antiquity*, vol. 23, 1957

124 Engl, Liselotte, *Die Traumgesichte des Inca Huayna Capac. Peru und Ecuador im XV. und XVI. Jahrhundert* (in preparation)

125 Engl, Liselotte, *Huayna Capac, Atahualpa und Huascar. Untersuchungen zur Geschichte der letzten Jahrzehnte des Inkareiches* (University thesis), 1954

126 Hagen, V. W. von, *Die Wüstenkönigreiche Perus*, Munich, 1966

127 Hagen, V. W. von, *Realm of the Incas*, New York, 1957

128 *Handbook of South-American Indians*, vol. 2: *The Andean Civilizations*, Washington, 1946. Edited by J. H. Steward, with contributions by Wendell C. Bennett, Rafael Larco Hoyle, Louis E. Valcarcel, John Howland Rowe, and others

129 Horkheimer, H., *Nahrung und Nahrungsgewinnung im vorspanischen Peru*. Biblioteca Ibero-Americana, vol. 2, Berlin, 1960

130 Karsten, R., *Das altperuanische Inkareich und seine Kultur*, Leipzig, 1949

131 Kauffmann-Doig, F., *El Perú antiguo*, Lima, 1963

132 Kauffmann-Doig, F., *Los fundamentos de la investigación del Perú arqueológico*, Lima, 1963

133 Kauffmann-Doig, F., *Origen de la cultura peruana*, Lima, 1963

134 Kauffmann-Doig, F., J. M. Valega and others, *Historia del Perú desde sus origines hasta el presente*, 3 vols., Lima, 1962–63

135 Kroeber, A. L., *Paracas Cavernas and Chavín*. University of California Publications in American Archeology and Ethnology, vol. 40, Berkeley and Los Angeles, 1953

136 Kutscher, G., *Chimu, eine altperuanische Hochkultur*, Berlin, 1950

137 Larco Hoyle, R., *Los Mochicas*, 2 vols., Lima, 1938–40

138 Larco Hoyle, R., *Cronología arqueológica del norte del Perú*, Trujillo and Buenos Aires, 1948

139 Larco Hoyle, R., *Checan, Studie über erotische Darstellungen in der peruanischen Kunst*, Munich, Geneva, Paris, 1965

140 Leuzinger, E., *Die Kunst von Alt-Peru*. Catalogue, Kunsthaus Zürich. Alt-Peru aus Schweizer Sammlungen, 1957

141 Lothrop, S. K., *Inca Treasure as Depicted by Spanish Historians*, Los Angeles, 1938

142 Mason, A. J., *The Ancient Civilization of Peru*, London, 1957

143 Posnansky, Arthur, *Die erotischen Keramiken der Mochicas und deren Beziehungen zu okzipital deformierten Schädeln*, Frankfort/Main, 1925

144 Sawyer, A. R., *The Nathan Cummings Collection of Ancient Peruvian Art*, Chicago, The Art Institute, 1954

145 Sawyer, A. R., *Tiahuanaco Tapestry*. The Textile Museum, 1962

146 Trimborn, H., *Die Kulturen Alt-Amerikas (Südamerika)*. In: *Handbuch zur Kulturgeschichte*, Constance, 1965

147 Ubbelohde-Doering, H., *Alt-Mexikanische und Peruanische Malerei*. In: *Meisterwerke aussereuropäischer Malerei*, pp. 297–336, Berlin, 1959

148 Ubbelohde-Doering, H., *Kunst im Reich der Inka*, Tübingen, 1952

149 Uhle, M., *Wesen und Ordnung der altperuanischen Kultur*. After Uhle's death edited by G. Kutscher, Berlin, 1959

150 Willey, G. R., *A Middle Period Cemetery in the Virú Valley, Northern Peru*. In: *Journal of the Washington Academy of Sciences*, vol. 37, No. 2, Washington, 1947

Chihuahua

Mexico

Rio Grande

Mississippi

Key Marcos

Cuba

Huaxtecs

Jalisco
Jalisco   Aztecs
Tarascans
Michoacán
Colima
Michoacán
Guerrero

Tula   El Tajín   Totonacs
Teotihuacán   Olmecs
Texcoco
Toluca   Mexico   Veracruz
Puebla   Comalcalco
Xochicalco   Tuxtla   Tabasco
Monte Albán   Palenque
Oaxaca   Mitla
Mixtecs   Chiapas   Yaxchilán   Chamá
Zapotecs   Chiapas
Maya civilization   Kaminaljuyú
Lake Atitlán

Yucatán   Yucatán
Jaina   Uxmal   Chichen Itzá
Kabáh   Mayapán   Cozumel
Sayil   Labná   Tulum
Campeche

Maya
Peten
Peten
Tikal
Quirigua
Piedras Negras   Copán
Ulua R.
Honduras

Guatemala

Pipiles   San Salvador

El Salvador   Nicaragua

Chorotegs   San José
Nicoya R.   Cocle   Colon
Costa Rica   Veraguas
Chiriquis   Panamá
Panama

Gulf of
Maracaibo

Tairona

Venezuela

Chibcha (Muiscas)

Chancay R.
Rio Magdalena
Quimbayas   Bogotá

Popayan   San Agustín   Colombia

Esmeraldas R.

Quito   Ecuador

Amazon R.

Central Andes

Brazil

Vicús
Mochicas
Lambayeque   Peru
Cupisnique
Chan-Chan   Recuay
Trujillo   Moche
Chavín de Huántar

Urubamba R.
Incas
Machu Picchu

Lima   Cuzco
Pachacamac   Chincha R.
Huari
Parecas   Ica R.   Ica
Lake Titicaca
La P
Tiahuanaco

Chile

Clay statuette
with two faces (detail),
so-called type
"Pretty Lady"
(see Ill. 7).

I

Seated woman. The clothing of the women in pre-classic times was still simple. First importance was given to hairdressing and headdress; among the many thousands of offerings found in graves were hardly any representations of two women with the same coiffure.

Female Dancer. Her attire consists only of a short skirt. As with all small clay figures of the pre-classic time, here too, the hair is dressed with particular care.

4

Fragment of a female figure. The original painting of the face and the hair dyed with cinnabar has been very well preserved for more than two thousand years.

Seated mother holding her child. This clay sculpture was found in Tlapacoya, opposite Tlatilco across the lake. In style the figures are similar to finds in Tlatilco, but not so far as quality is concerned.

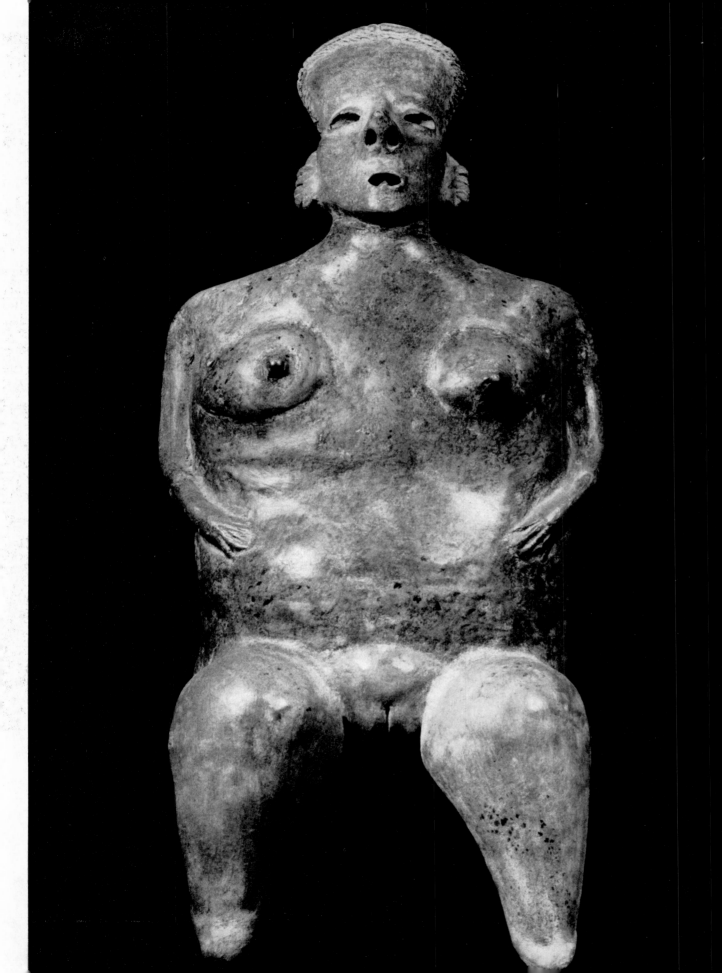

24

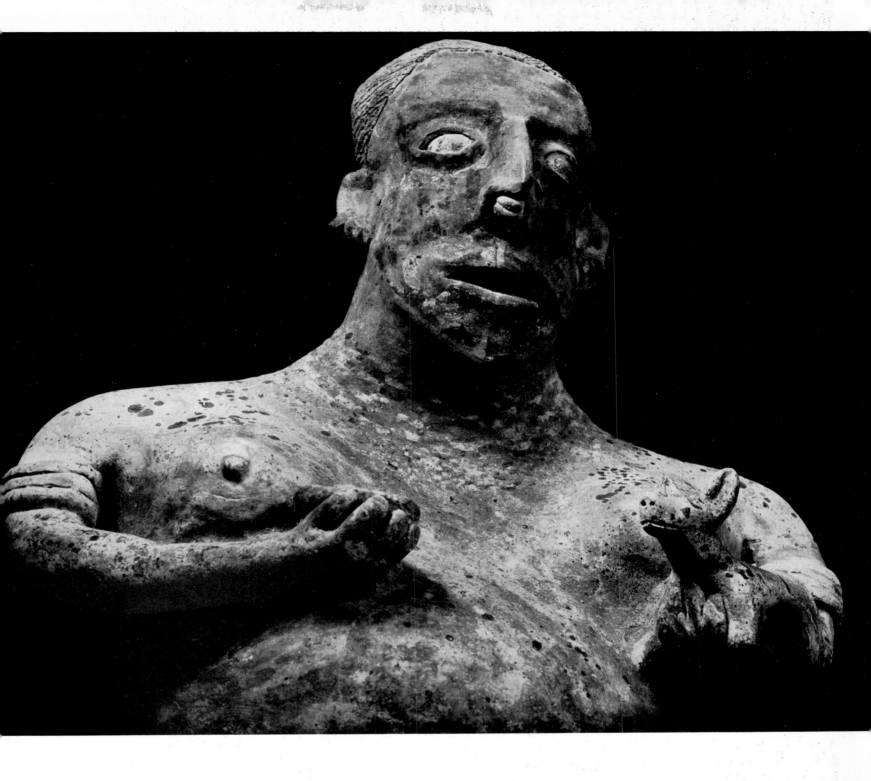

Seated naked woman. She holds her hands over her belly; her only ornaments are ear rings.

Noble lady with a little dog in one hand and a cup in the other. As ornament she wears a nose ring.

Recumbent, probably pregnant, woman in the form of a vessel. This was a common method of making ceramics, as the wire framework used today by ceramic workers was unknown, and it was impossible to fire solid figures of this large size.

Seated naked woman holding her hands over her belly. She, too, wears the ear rings or clips typical of the Nayarit region. The broad cheekbones, and the modelling around the eyes in figures of this kind lead some experts to speak of a Mongoloid type.

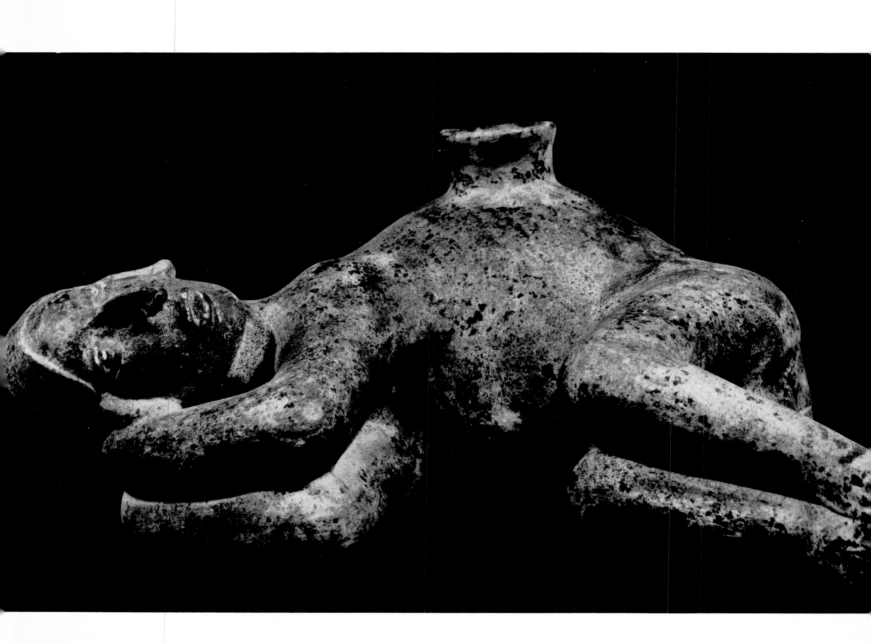

27

Seated woman of the so-called Mongoloid type. She wears what
suggests a divided skirt, probably only because the artist wanted
to avoid moulding a clay skirt, which would have been too fragile.
In contrast to pre-classic times, the classic period shows a loss in
the importance of individualized representation of the hairdressing,
greater value being then attached to the painting of the face and
of the body, and to tattooed designs.

Vessel shaped as a pregnant woman, made of blackish-grey clay.

Vessel shaped as a resting young girl or young woman. This vessel has probably never been used. The artist chose the shape of a vessel so as to obtain the cavity required in the process of firing.

Seated young woman. Here the artist had made an opening at the back of the head to let the hot air escape. Like all ceramics of the civilizations of the northwest coast, this one is rather expressionistic and little attention is given to detail.

Clay figure, representing a recumbent, pregnant woman.

Couple on a seat. The man wears a loincloth and a sash or belt; the woman is dressed in a kind of shawl worn around her hips. Both wear armlets and the usual ornaments in the ears; but the chain with a pendant indicating a pectoral—usually the token worn by male dignitaries—is in this sculpture the prerogative of the woman.

Clay figure of a young deity. Around her headdress and her waist are entwined snakes, attributes of the rain god. This figure probably represents a variation of the goddess Coatlicue, the "Goddess with the skirt of snakes," also called the "Filth-eater." She was the goddess of the earth and of fertility. This clay figure comes from the region of the central Gulf coast and dates back to approximately seven centuries before the Aztec civilization reached its apex.

Small clay fragment representing a mother with her child. As is customary sometimes even today, the child was carried on the back of the mother in a large wrap (rebozo).

View of the 65 m. high Sun Pyramid of Teotihuacán, the centre of the greatest theocratic civilization of Mexican antiquity.

The water goddess Chalchiuhtlicue, the "Lady with the skirt of jade." She was the goddess of the streams and rivers and the sister-wife of the rain god Tlaloc; she was said to possess youthful beauty and liveliness. She symbolized youth, was moody and ostentatious, and her attire was that of a noblewoman. This image is carved in chalcedony, a kind of alabaster found in some parts of Mexico.

Realistic stone sculpture of a humpbacked old woman.

Mictlanciuatl, the goddess of death, is shown here as the apparition of death, as that of the universal destroyer.

Statue of Coatlicue, the goddess of the earth and of death, is represented here as giving birth to everything and devouring everything. As Cipactli she was a monster, which devoured all living things and also the stars. She was the original symbol of discord, supposed to be the mother of Huitzilopochtli, the Aztecs' god of war. She was the monster who swallowed up the sun in the evening and brought it forth again in the morning. The image is quite contrary to our idea of divine beauty.

Head of the moon goddess Coyolxauhqui, "She with the golden bells." She was the sister of Tezcatlipoca, "Smoking Mirror," who was a war god of the Aztecs and represented the North. The goddess was never shown as a whole figure, probably because the moon, too, was seen as a bodiless being.

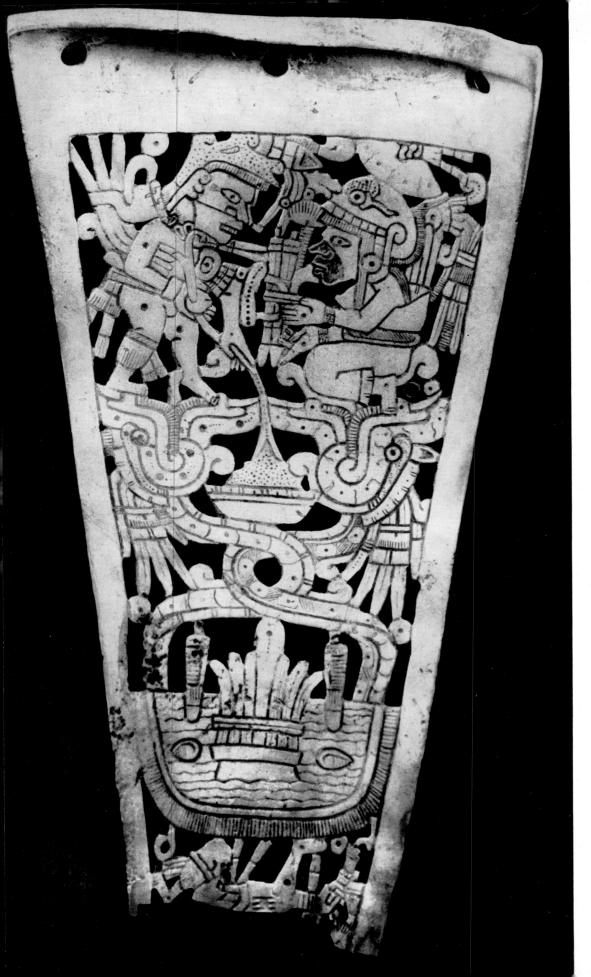

Pendant showing two rain deities at their religious activities; Tlaloc, "He who makes sprout," and Chalchiuhtlicue, the "Lady with the skirt of jade."

Stone sculpture of the goddess Tlazoltéotl, the goddess of the earth and of birth. She is shown giving birth to a child.

Fragment of the head of the maize goddess Chicomecóatl. Although for the Indians maize was the most essential food, this highly important deity was very seldom represented. Above her human face seven corn cobs are moulded as her headdress.

Statue of the goddess Coatlicue, the goddess of death and of the earth. She is the "Goddess with the skirt of snakes," shown here as an old woman with a death's head. She is hewn out of a basalt block, and her dress is decorated with inlaid work of turquoise and mother-of-pearl.

Straight, tall beaker with highly stylized design of dancers or couples of lovers. The upper and the lower edge are surrounded by mouldings of hieroglyph-like ornaments, which, however, have a solely decorative significance.

Cup of clay with a highly stylized female figure, probably a priestess or goddess. This type of ceramics is, in style, akin to the objects from Honduras, shown above. There is also some resemblance to the painting of vessels in the lowlands of Guatemala. It is, however, not yet possible to determine the exact period, pending thorough scholarly excavations in the region of the present-day Republic of El Salvador. There does not seem to be any near connection with the classic Maya civilization, as the delicate drawings (for example, skirt and bonnet) have a kind of hieroglyphic character, but are not identical with the hieroglyphs of the classic Maya civilization.

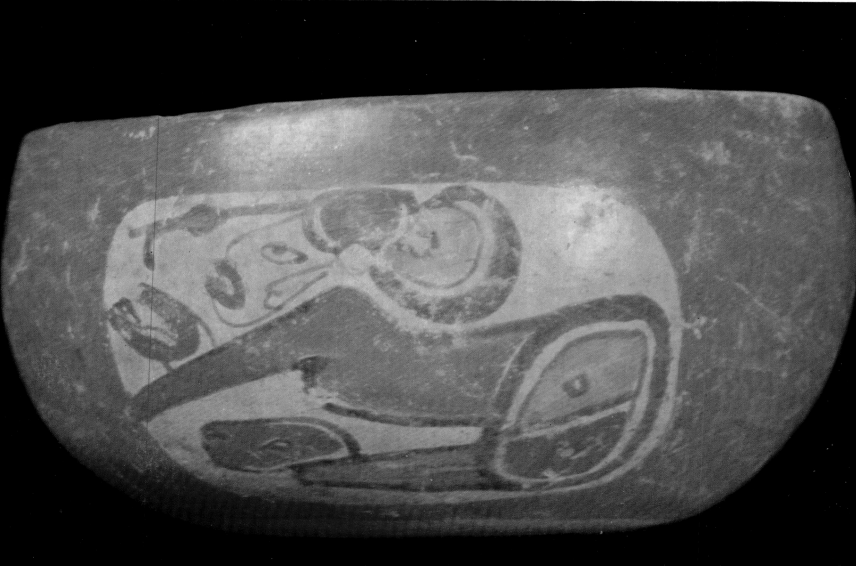

Female figures shown on plate 18 of the Maya Manuscript kept in Dresden. This plate belongs to a series of illustrated calendar pages which probably formed a kind of fortune-telling almanac. These pages mainly are concerned with women's questions which is shown by the numerous representations of female deities, in particular that of the moon goddess who was the patroness of female handicrafts, but likewise of medicine, pregnancy and birth.

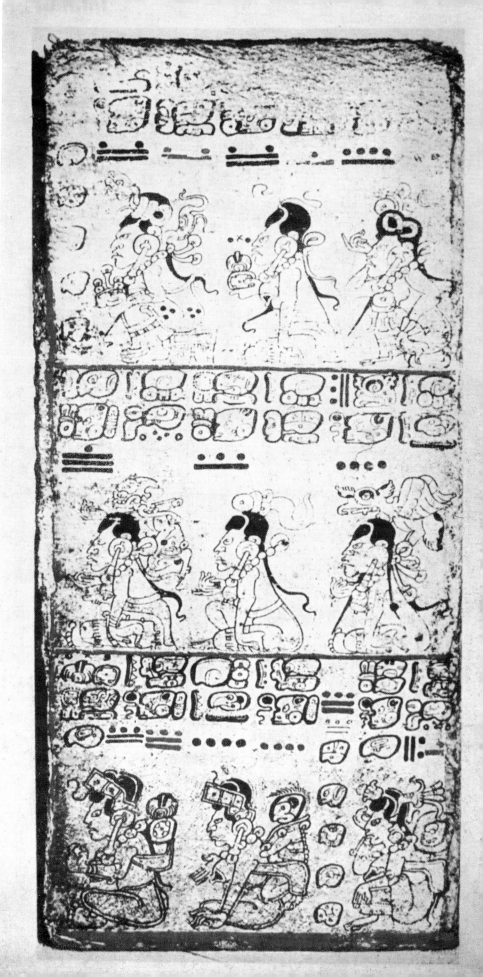

Clay fragment of the head of a young girl, with carefully moulded hairdressing. It probably is the representation of a simple woman, as she is not wearing any ornaments in her ears. It came from the highlands of Chiapas. This region on the western border of the Maya civilization has, like the other border regions, taken only a slight share in the cultural progress of the lowlands.

Sculpture representing the standing figure of a young girl. The original meaning of this early and still primitive work can only be guessed at. It was certainly the requirements of ancient fertility cults, which frequently induced the primitive tillers of the soil to make these archaic female figures. All through the pre-classic time little female figures of this kind were made in Mesoamerica. Whether offerings from graves, or votive pictures found in the fields into which they had been dug, these small figures after thousands of years are now once more gradually seeing the light of day. The expert can place them geographically by their different coiffures, the planes of the face around the eyes and by the various, very cleverly placed depressions which mark the pupils and give meaning to the look. In addition to the frequently very refined coiffure, the clothing consists at most of a loincloth, a small necklace and large earplugs.

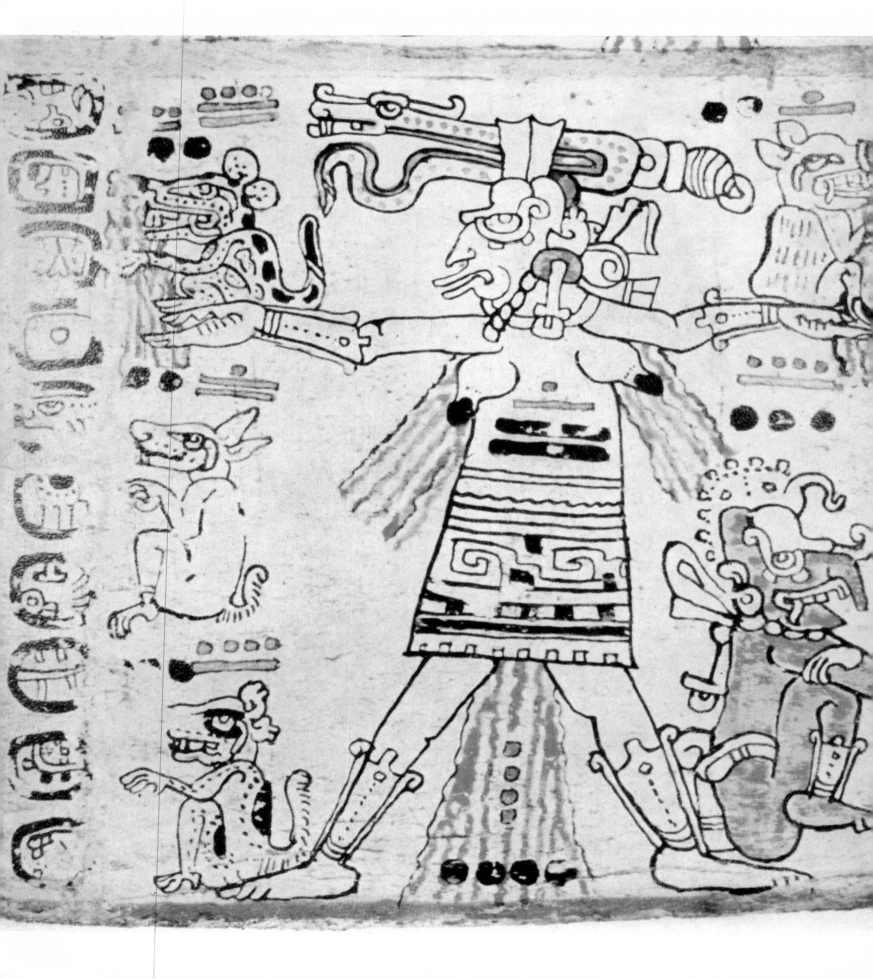

The goddess Ixchel. She was the mother or grandmother of the gods, the mistress of births, and the patron of female handicraft. She had, however, also negative, misanthropic traits; she was thought to be responsible for floods and storms. Her shrine was on the Island of Cozumel. The illustration is taken from the Codex Tro-Cortesianus (Codex Madrid). With its 112 pages this "folding book" is the largest of the three known items of Maya literature.

Wall paintings in the "Temple of Frescoes" of Tulum showing the deity Itzamná. The style of these frescoes is influenced by the Mixtec style and shows only a slight resemblance to the wall paintings of the classic Maya civilization.

Vessel shaped as a resting woman, with a jug on her shoulders. Her parted hair falls down to her lap. By somehow fusing carrier and burden the artist has succeeded in creating a very vivid impression. Although this figure measures only a few centimetres, it seems almost monumental.

Vessel shaped as a seated woman, perhaps pregnant. The woman holds a jug in her hands.

Fragment showing a noblewoman with necklace, earplugs and nose ornament. Beads and earplugs, like those indicated here, were made by the Mayas of jade, a material they valued more than gold.

Detail of Stele H, forming part of the main group. It is dated 9.17.12.0.0.0.4 Ahau 14 Muan (782). This masterpiece seems to be the only one among the many steles of Copán to represent a female being. She is clothed in the skin of a jaguar, splendidly ornamented, and showing the special ceremonial decorations appropriate to the highest dignitaries. Under the stele there was found as an offering a necklace of jadeite beads with a small, thin gold plate as pendant. This is the only piece of gold that has so far been found in connection with a dated Maya monument; it was imported from Panama or Costa Rica.

Rattle showing an old man with a young woman in a costly dress. The old man wears a helmet of feathers and a loincloth (called "ex"); on his chest he has a woven or embroidered ornament. Both figures are adorned with earplugs. The young lady holds a fan in her hand. She wears a blouse called "kub" and a long skirt called "pic." In addition she has a long coat-like wrap.

Woman seated on a bench.

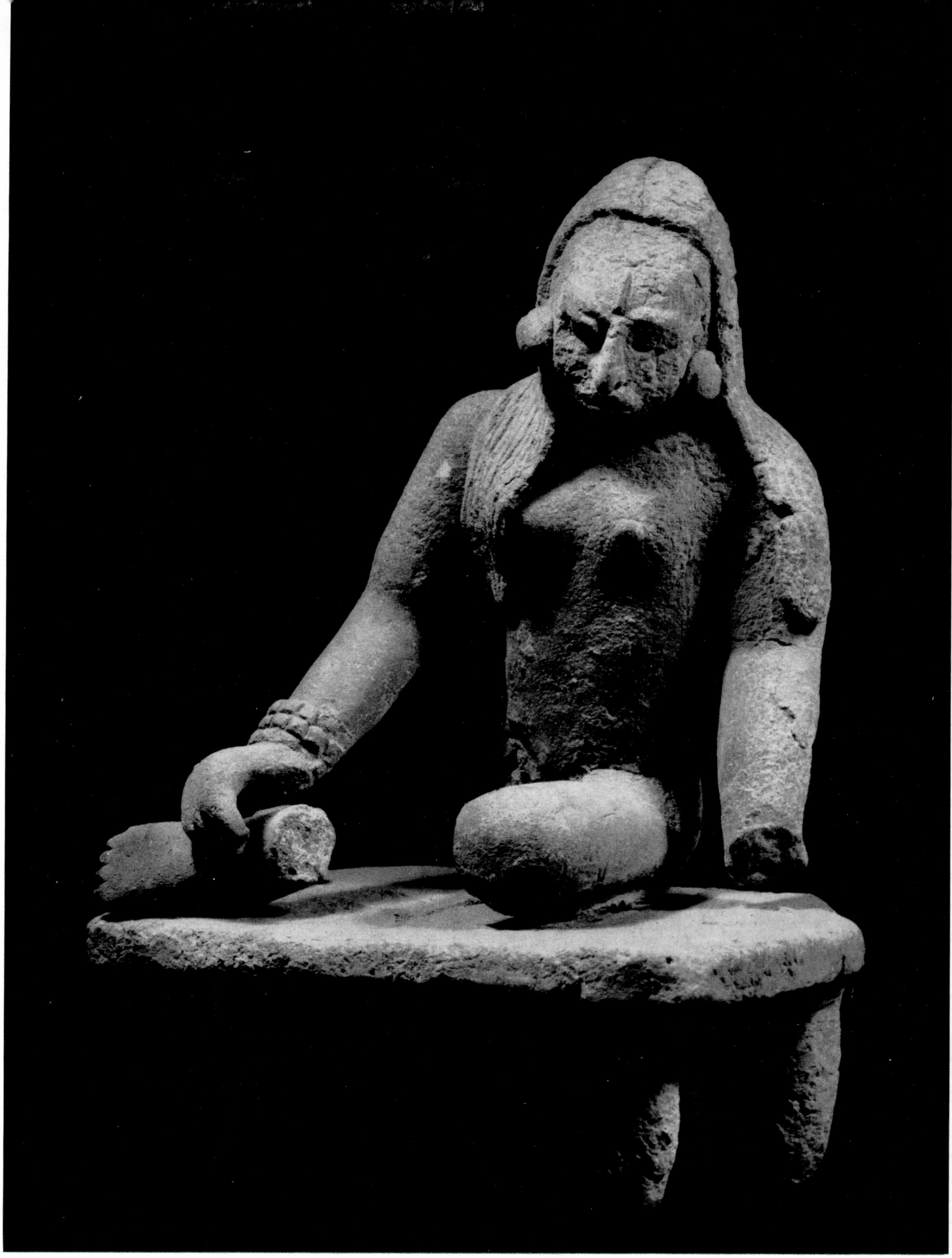

Ocarina shaped as a richly clothed lady, her hands raised. With her costly dress she wears strings of beads and large earplugs.

Ocarina shaped as a deity in festive attire, or a high priest representing the deity. Perhaps the figure is standing at the throne, or it is only some wooden construction to be carried on the back.

Noble lady with dwarf. This frequently appearing theme and the fact that the great pyramid of Uxmal was called "House of the Dwarf" hint at a now forgotten legend.

Sumptuously clothed lady in ceremonial attire and jewelry. Hardly at any other time, and hardly in any other region, has such great importance been attached to the appearance of small works of art as to that of the Jaina terracotta grave-offerings.

Ocarina shaped as a lewd old man and a young girl. This theme, known not alone to the Maya Indians, appears so frequently among the Jaina terracottas that one is inclined to think it is inspired by a popular ancient legend.

Courting couple. Both wear high hats, ruffles round the neck and ornaments of beads. The woman is clothed in a skirt, held together by a magnificent belt-buckle, while the man wears a loincloth.

Ocarina shaped as a noble lady. She is accompanied by a man with the head of a coyote or at least masked as an animal. Probably this is the illustration of an ancient legend. She lovingly embraces the zoomorphic being, which is adorned with valuable jewelry.

Noble lady. At her feet lies a dwarf-like man or a child. So far it is unknown whether this frequently recurring theme referred to some legend or was meant to indicate the lady's superior rank.

Mother with children preparing tortillas (maize cakes). This image is exceptional among the Jaina terracottas. Usually only priests, highly placed warriors or noble ladies were represented; such offerings hardly ever referred to everyday life.

Small figure of standing woman, possibly a symbol of fertility. The figure overemphasizes the importance of the hips and shoulders. The artist did without any delicate details which would have been too difficult to achieve in this porous and brittle clay. As Venezuela is, from the archaeological point of view, still fairly new ground, the place of discovery and the age of such objects can be ascertained only by comparison with similar pieces found elsewhere.

Naked seated woman. As headdress she wears a bonnet decorated with geometrical designs. Her jewelry consists of a necklace of beads and of two ear rings. The clay is painted red, but is of such poor quality that the artist did not take much trouble over any individual features. The figure came from Nicaragua, a country which until now has been almost ignored by archaeologists.

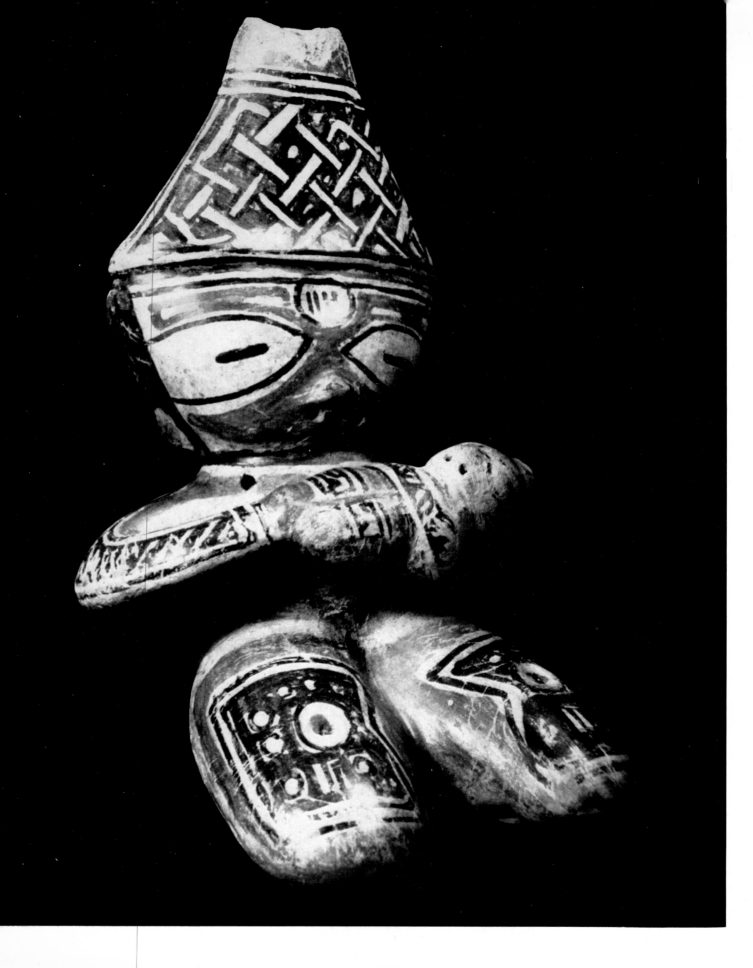

Mother carrying her child in her arms. This figure of very well fired clay, with brilliant paint, chiefly orange, red and cocoa-brown, is worked as a flute with a loop for carrying; it came from the border between Nicaragua and Costa Rica.

Two seated women, their hands at their hips.

Vessel shaped as a seated woman. The figure is so highly stylized, as to be nearly square; the face— like the whole body—is extremely flat. Armlets and anklets are only slightly indicated. The figure shows irregular perforations.

A bas-relief of this stele shows a female deity with the teeth of a beast of prey. Two earplugs give to the overlarge head a square shape. The body and the raised hands are of secondary importance. This sacred stele stands in the vicinity of San Agustín, an important centre of a past civilization. The Second World War, financial difficulties and the subsequent political unrest in Colombia have so far prevented any intensive excavations at this important site, which extends to more than fifty square kilometres.

Front and back of a standing female figure from Costa Rica. The only part completed by the artist in detail is the long hair falling down over the neck.

Standing female figure. Breast and upper arms are tattooed with an arched pattern of regular scars. The left forearm is broken off.

So-called ceremonial knife with highly stylized figure of fertility goddess from Colombia.

Gold amulet showing a two-headed deity, cast by the lost way. According to the Indians' belief, who lived on the coasts of the Isthmus of Darién, these amulets were very efficacious with regard to fertility. Probably worn by men as well as by women, they were also put as offerings into the graves.

The needles are made of cactus thorns and carved hardwood, the spinning whorl consists of clay and shows remains of wool and cotton threads. Like the sewing box depicted on the same page, they belonged to the offerings found in a woman's grave.

Wooden box (sewing box) with geometrical motifs, a receptacle for wool, needles, thread and spinning whorls.

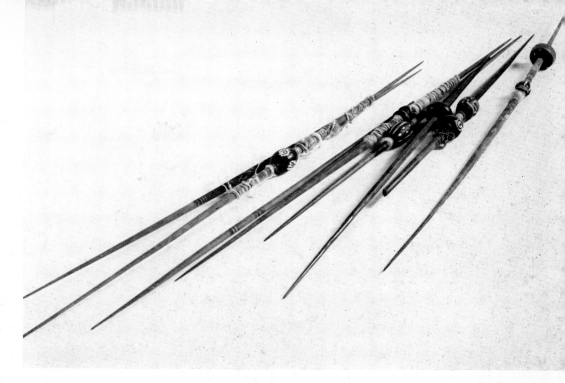

101

Large vessel of clay. Above, a group of figures probably representing a member of the upper ranks of the population with his wives and a llama. The body of the vessel is decorated with a frieze showing stylized beasts of prey in negative painting.

Vessel representing a family in their home. The man holds a large vessel in his hands. A small rather superficially modelled monkey, characteristic of vessels of the Chimu style, sits on the handle of the spout.

A couple of lovers separately modelled, sit on a bulbous vessel of clay with spout and bow-shaped handle.

Bulbous vessel of clay representing a woman carrying a heavy burden by means of a headband. The head is moulded so as to be prominent and to show the huge strain involved. By contrast the body is modelled only in relief.

In a stylized mountain landscape stands a demon or priest with the mask of a deity. He is apparently judging a fettered naked prisoner or adulterer who is sitting below him to the right. To the left sits a woman in a checked dress, probably a witness. She carries a bundle on her back and has shut her eyes; she holds a vessel in her hands.

Upper part of a digger's spade or, according to other archaeologists, a sword of balsa wood. It shows a jaguar raping a naked, young woman (or sacrificing her). The jaguar played a dominant role in nearly all high civilizations of both Americas and was even worshipped as a god. It is therefore likely that some religious conception underlay the scene represented here.

Doll made of raw cotton, threads of wool and woven tapestry. As less workmanlike care was bestowed on this kind of doll than on the "mantas" it may be assumed that they were real toys, given to children at their burial.

This embroidered cotton fabric forms part of a shroud ("manta") in which mummies were wrapped. From ancient Peru the most beautiful and oldest woven materials have come down to us, showing nearly all kinds of weaving known today and 190 color shades.

Vessel representing a seated woman wearing a knotted dress. The tube-shaped spout is connected by the handle with the woman's head. As with all vessels of the Nazca civilization, sculpture takes second place to the art of painting. Dress and arms shown on the body of the vessel are not carved but painted.

Fragment of a vessel with handle, showing an erotic scene. Representations of this kind are very frequent in the civilization of Moche, contrasting with the other styles of art in pre-Spanish history. The artists from Moche probably knew no prudishness in the sense of Christian-Occidental conceptions; usually they added a sleeping child as member of the family to their pictures of erotic scenes.

Vessel with handle representing a couple joined in a kiss of the tongues. The figures are so neutral, have so little body, that possibly it may not be the representation of an erotic scene but a symbolic image of the joining of two kinds of field produce.

Page 112
Mummy of a noble female in magnificent setting from the necropolis of Paracas.